# STOP WISHING
# START CREATING

**Stop Wishing Start Creating: 7 Step Blueprint to Manifesting Your Life**

ISBN 978-1-7334995-4-5 (paperback)

Subjects: Self-realization/Self help/Motivational & Inspirational/Personal Growth

Any internet references included in this book are current at the time of publication but may change over time. Please refer to www.GertrudeMarie.com for updated sources.

# ACKNOWLEDGEMENTS

To my three amazing kids, my inspiration and great love.

To my mom for teaching me that there are no limits but the ones that we set for ourselves, and for speaking to me the language of manifestation as I grew up.

To my dad for teaching me to think and question, to make lists and plan. For setting an example of integrity and resilience and for always believing in me.

To my brother, thank you for always having my back, and for the fascinating conversations about the many passions that we share.

To Helga and Erwin, for lovingly supporting us and helping us make our dreams come true.

To my grandmother, for her loving guidance and teaching me about the Law of Attraction before it was common knowledge.

To my aunts, uncles, and grandparents who have always been there for me, and are still supporting me from heaven.

To my amazing friends that are like family to- me, and my cherished students that have motivated me to write this book.

All my gratitude to you, my beloved reader. A book only fulfills its purpose when it is read. Thank you for allowing my writing to achieve its mission ☺

As a token of appreciation, I want to give you a free guided meditation to assist you in raising your vibration and making meditation very easy and straightforward for you.

You can download it here:
https://www.gertrudemarie.com/free-guided-meditations

# Table of Contents

# FOREWORD

I intend for this book to help anchor light into the planet by recalling the amazing light you brought to the world when you were born and the massive power you possess to create the life that you want. I want to ignite the spark that starts a complete transformation in you. When you look back on this day, you will remember this was the moment you decided to take your life into your own hands and started co-creating with the universe. By the law of attraction, your desire to create a higher reality brought this book to you. Isn't it amazing? Please acknowledge how amazingly unique and special you are, because when you do, you will be able to transform whatever might be obstructing you from manifesting your heart's desires. Soon, you will be able to shine your light freely and help remind others to shine theirs. Soon, you'll be able to create a life beyond your wildest dreams!

*Let gratitude be the motor of your creations*

*Lord, make me an instrument of Thy Peace*
*Where there is hatred, let me sow love;*
*Where there is injury, pardon;*
*Where there is doubt, faith*
*Where there is despair, hope;*
*Where there is darkness, light;*
*Where there is sadness, joy.*

*Oh, Divine Master,*
*Grant that I may not so much seek*
*To be consoled as to console;*
*To be understood as to understand;*
*To be loved as to love;*
*For it is in giving that we receive,*
*It is in pardoning that we are pardoned,*
*It is in dying that we are born into eternal life.*

*Saint Francis de Assisi*

*You are the author of your story so think to create,*
*feel to attract, imagine to transform.*

# INTRODUCTION

Good things don't just come to special people. Each of us arrives to this planet fully equipped with the skills, talent, strength, and power to create unlimited good in our lives and the lives of those around us. We have been given everything that we need to manifest anything we desire. It's just a matter of deciding to stop crossing our fingers and becoming deliberate creators.

This book will help you attract a reality beyond your wildest dreams. Whether you have already started your path to joy and high vibration life or you are new to the subject, this is the roadmap for attracting the life your heart desires.

Just imagine: what if what your heart desires became realized with ease? What if you could live the life of your dreams? What if you could unleash such strong energy capable of making your dreams come true? What if you could delegate all the hard work while you were enjoying the fun part? What if you could achieve all of this regardless of your life's circumstances right now?

There's a simple recipe for this—a series of steps that can take you from where you are right now to where you want to go.

What I present in this book is a powerful and effective process that I have assembled in the course of more than 15 years, derived from my own experience as well as that of the people and groups I have worked with.

I have personally manifested amazing things in my life like houses, trips, situations, businesses, opportunities, gifts, and the success of this book, which is the result of the steps included in this book.

Some people might think I have an extraordinary gift and the fact is I do, but WE ALL DO!

We all have immense creative power within us, capable of bending reality and shaping our lives. We just need to unleash it. And although I share some of my own experiences, this book is not about me but about all the people who have benefited from this program. It has been the positive feedback and requests to publish it as a manual that moved me to create this book.

I include examples of people using these steps and getting amazing results not only because I get so excited when I hear their success stories, but because it will help you realize that you, too, can be a part of these success stories.

Of course, it doesn't mean that just by reading the book you'll magically transform your life. You have to apply the steps to your life. You have to actually do something. When you do, your life will begin changing for the better. This is a proven method that has been tried so many times with great results.

This book will provide you with a seven-step attractor blueprint that will help you get from a point of wishing to a point of becoming a deliberate co-creator with the universe and attracting all that your heart desires into your life.

Manifesting should be fun, easy and exciting, so in each chapter I have included a section called LET'S PLAY! that's designed for you to practice the teachings of each chapter, so you start building confidence with your manifesting abilities.

I invite you to relax, take a deep breath, open yourself to infinite possibilities, and begin the journey to your new and amazing life. Remember that the journey of a thousand miles begins with one single step. This book is a big step for you. Congratulations!

Make sure to go to the end of the book where you'll find a section with all the steps put together. You can also find a link to download a free manifestation play sheet.

# ATTRACTOR STEP 1

# KNOW, FLOW
# AND ALLOW

# ATTRACTOR STEP 1
## KNOW, FLOW AND ALLOW

Life is about experiences and what we learn from them. We're born to grow and evolve. Our hopes and dreams are the roadmaps for our life's purpose. Everything that we want to attract to our life is usually because deep within, it has something that our soul wants to experience. Just like we are provided with books and supplies when we go to school, the universe provides us with everything that we need to have a learning experience in life. Manifestation may seem magic but it's an intrinsic part of all of us; we were all given a powerful "magic wand" to manifest our heart's desire. Everything is available to us. We just need to ask for it. However, to ask for something, you should first know what you want. That is why the first step to attract the life of your dreams is to understand what the life of your dreams looks like, and decide what you want to focus on. It might seem obvious, but sometimes in the manifestation process, we may feel stuck, not knowing what we want.

For me, that moment of feeling stuck happened one day in the spring of 2003. That day I was driving to the gym as usual. Little did I know how special this day would become. It started a chain reaction of events that would literally change my life.

In fact, it began several months before, when I was in the ultrasound room with Andres, my husband, and my oldest son, waiting to see the sonogram image of the four-month baby I was pregnant with.

To our shock and surprise, the only thing we were able to see was a baby that was dead. The technician could not answer any questions but instead went out of the room and came back with the doctor who explained that the baby had not survived.

This was supposed to be a very exciting moment, and as you can imagine, the news was nothing short of devastating. This was a very intense experience, especially since I had already had two miscarriages. But this time was even more challenging because my pregnancy was already very advanced. I had thought that by hitting the fourth month of pregnancy, my baby would be safe. By then everyone knew I was pregnant and having to bring the news and explain what happened to everyone was even more devastating.

I cried unrestrained each day after dropping my son to pre-school and this went on for weeks. I was dragging through my days with an immense sense of emptiness and sadness. Was it my fault? Did I do something wrong? I felt so sad and confused. It was hard to appreciate all the blessings in my life. But one morning after a dream I had, I realized all the things I'd taken for granted: my wonderful son, my loving and supportive husband, my amazing family, and the fact that I was healthy to enjoy all of this.

That's when my journey to change my life began. I started going to the gym every day. I read as many spiritual and motivational books as I could. I started a meditation practice and decided to try some concepts I had learned as a teenager. I needed a change. I wanted to turn my life around. After almost a year of using different tools and techniques, I could see a big change in me, but I still felt like something was missing. It felt like I had just completed a puzzle but had lost the last piece not even knowing what that piece looked like.

I wanted to know what that piece was but I didn't know how to find that out. At that time, a friend of mine was reading a book on intention so I decided I'd give the concept a try. Off I went and set the intention to understand where that feeling of missing something was coming from. I had been meditating as a daily practice but this time I meditated with that intention. Finally, after several days, the moment came. It was about getting insight and knowing what I wanted. I was doing my daily routine when all of a sudden it all became so clear to me. I had a spark of inspiration to share all the tools that I had used to turn my life around.

And that was what that day at the gym was all about. I didn't know at that moment, but the process I was creating would change not only my live but also other's lives as well.

At first I was concerned about how I would be able to do it. I was worried that maybe I wasn't prepared for the role. I worried what people would think of me. I had so many reasons not to follow my inner guidance and at the same time I felt like I needed to follow my intuition. So I set the intention to clear my fears and gain clarity. That turned things around for me, I felt inspired and empowered, ready to start this new path. I'd made a shift in my life that would allow me to help others create a positive change in their lives as well, and it all started when I knew what I wanted to do. Once I knew what I wanted, I set my intention and things started rolling.

Intention is the power to focus your mind. It is the force that allows you to accomplish what could otherwise seem impossible.

Everything starts with a desire that triggers an intention. When you decide to send a text to a friend, go to the fridge to get something to eat, or even just to stretch your body, you start with a desire that unleashes an intention.

When we have an intention, we've chosen the outcome we want to experience. A clear intention makes the universe align to bring us what we want.

On the other hand, will or desire is the relentless force that makes you act to accomplish what you want.

Intention and will are fundamental in the Law of Attraction process.

Intention is the seed, your consciousness is the soil, and your will is the water and sun that helps the seed grow. Without seed, there's no plant, but at the same time, if you leave the seed in your pocket it still won't grow. It's when you consciously place your intention out to the universe that your will works to create that which your heart desires. A seed that is planted, watered

14

and cared for will reap a beautiful plant. The more conscious you are about your intention, the more powerful it will be.

I was born into a family of entrepreneurs and one thing that I liked about Andres when we met was that he shared my wild and crazy passion for business ideas. So even before we got married, we started our first business. We earned some money but it was not yet substantial. As time passed, it became too stressful and finally we decided to close the business and take the safer route. I began work with my dad, and Andres obtained a job at a large international corporation. While still at our jobs, we tested starting other businesses but neither of them took off like we'd hoped; however, there was an internal itch, that motor that kept pushing us toward the entrepreneurial road. We tried so many ideas, some were good and others not so much but at that point, none of our businesses were very successful.

As a teenager, I had learned law of attraction concepts that were my life's motto. My grandmother taught me about the power of visualization, my dad asked me to write down the top ten things I wanted in life, and my mother told me that the universe was a mirror that would reflect my thoughts and actions. These were powerful concepts for me to understand, but for some strange reason, in my adult life, I had unconsciously drawn a line between my spiritual-everyday life and my businesses. As I was trying to control the outcome of a project, not allowing the universe to do its part, I would usually feel stuck and stressed. It was as if making money was not part of my spiritual path or there was something morally wrong about manifesting business opportunities or wealth. It was when I opened myself to the idea that abundance has many faces and that there's more than enough to go around , that my businesses had a major leap. That was the moment I decided to embrace all areas of my life as part of my divine purpose and everything started working out in miraculous ways.

When we do what makes us happy, what gives us real joy, we start manifesting at a faster rate because we become aligned with our higher purpose and connected to our higher will.

Your higher purpose is the highest possible outcome for your life while your higher will is the force that helps you act in alignment with your divine plan, and when you work in line with these two powerful forces, you become a "factory" of miracles.

We come to this world equipped with everything we need to fulfill our smallest and largest missions.

We often think that our mission needs to be something huge, like saving the world from greed, finding a way to end hunger or eradicating poverty. Because we don't see the whole picture, it is hard for us to realize that a teacher, a host at a restaurant, and the president of a country all have equally important missions.

From working with clients, I have discovered that one of the most important purposes of our life is not what we accomplish in the physical world. It is the learning that we carry with us when we cross over. We learn easy lessons such as being more organized, loving unconditionally, being independent, being strong and working together.

We have the desire to accomplish, because at a soul level, our desire works like an engine that moves us toward that which will help us learn and evolve.

We are creators of our reality even when we are not aware of this principle. Manifesting is natural to us. Manifesting is the art of focusing our intention and allowing the universe to do the "hard work," not the other way around. We shouldn't struggle to get what we want because the universe contains all possibilities for us; the one you desire is already there waiting for you to ask for it.

You just need to know what you really want to create, and then align what you want with your Divine Purpose so that it is manifested for the highest good.

Meditation is a great practice to bring clarity and know what we want. Further in the book, I'll cover the meditation subject, but for now, just keep in mind that you can use it to be clear about what you want. When I want to set an intention and make sure it's aligned with my Higher purpose, I use meditation and it's a great tool. The first thing I do is to take a few deep breaths and then I set an objective for my meditation, which is usually to align my manifesting intention to my Higher Purpose. I even imagine a bright light above me radiating my Higher Purpose onto me. Then I start meditating. Right after meditation, I release my intention because on one hand the brain waves after meditation are ideal to program the subconscious mind and on the other the energetic frequency, the rate at which energy vibrates after meditation, is fertile soil to plant my intention seed.

We create through the frequency that we radiate and that frequency, as we'll see later in the book, is created by emotions, beliefs, thoughts, and words.

Another way to align your desires to your Divine Purpose is by connecting with your Soul, a part of you that holds the highest potential for your life and by asking the universe to bring something in a way that is for your highest good and that of all involved.

Life is not a series of random circumstances, but it is our consciousness that creates our life. In other words, we are the director of our life, co-creating reality by letting the universe know what we want. We communicate these desires every moment through our thoughts and the energy that those thoughts create.

Further in the book, I'll talk specifically about the power of our thoughts but for now, it is important to understand that our thoughts create emotions and emotions affect our energy system (chakras and aura, which will be covered in another chapter).

When our energy systems are in harmony, our desires are aligned with our higher will and our highest good. Therefore, even the desire for a new home or a better job teaches us something spiritually and helps us evolve.

If we allow our energy to become discordant, like the chakras being out of balance or our aura shrinking or becoming dull, it could become hard to distinguish our Higher Will and a lower feeling of wanting. We could want things that are not in the interest of our highest good nor the highest good of others.

A pure desire seeks the highest good for all. A lower feeling of wanting something doesn't include the highest good for all and the results are poor.

Taking care of our energy and being mindful of our thoughts, words, and intentions, is a simple way to strengthen the connection with our higher will and align our desires to it.

What is our Higher Self and how do we communicate with it?

Our Higher Self is an aspect of our Soul. It is the highest condition that we can achieve in our physical body in our lifetime. Our Higher Self is an intrinsic part of us, not a separate being. Our Higher Self is connected to divine purpose, divine intelligence, truth, and love. In other words, it is connected to All That Is.

Those feelings and thoughts that push us forward in peace and joy, come from our Higher Self. Hunches and gut feelings that elevate us and inspire us are also our Higher Self in action. It is not necessary to feel anything for our Higher Self or to feel the presence of our Higher Self.

It is important to distinguish between our ego-based thoughts and the inspiration from our Higher Self. There are some parameters to let you know if you are getting messages from your Higher Self, or if your ego is trying to protect itself from change.

## 1. Peace and Joy

The messages from your Higher Self and evolved beings, like Masters and Angels, are usually surrounded in light, peace, love, and joy. If you sense any unpleasant feeling or thought, it is not your Higher Self.

## 2. Empathy and Compassion.

The messages from your Higher Self are compassionate and empathetic with yourself and others. It motivates us to take care of ourselves while considering others with compassion.

## 3. Judgment Free

Our Higher Self communicates with compassion and from a high perspective, so it doesn't judge us or other people.

## 4. Positivity.

Our Higher Self has the highest vision of things and it communicates that vision to us, inspiring in us feelings of gratitude, beauty, wisdom, and wonder.

## 5. Wisdom and Strength

Because our Higher Self has the highest vision for us, it can communicate in a calm way that you need to change paths, establish boundaries or that simply what you are inquiring about, is a not for your best and highest good. However, remember that it will always come in a fear-free way.

The highest outcome in our life experience is to evolve and become our Higher Self. To strengthen the bond with our Higher Self, we only need a strong intention to embody it.

Once we know what our Higher Self is, then we can understand that the Higher Will is the purest form of personal choice and intent.

Aligning our will with the Higher Will, allows us to go with the flow, or in other words, let go and let God.

Life is like a river and we are sailing in our boats. When we're manifesting, there are times when we need to take control and row. However, other times we need to take advantage of the currents and just go with the flow. This is because if we try to row when the currents are strong, we will become exhausted, frustrated and will probably get stuck.

We are humans with expectations. We hope for outcomes but sometimes we hold on to them so strongly that it is like sailing on a boat and suddenly seeing a tree branch. If we stretch and hold on to it, we get stuck. The more we hold on to it, the less control we have over our boat. We may end up losing our boat and having to let go of the branch, to swim and catch up with our boat, after a lot of effort and suffering.

As I mentioned before, manifesting is in our nature and should be easy. We just need to set our intention and then let the universe bring what we want in the best way, form and time possible.

In situations where we are struggling, we often get attached either to a person, situation, relationship or an outcome. We get in our own way, obstructing the natural flow of energy. We can save ourselves a lot of suffering in those situations, by letting go of our expectations and letting the universe work out the best route for us.

Putting this in perspective, we create our reality with our thoughts, feelings, and words. The more we embody our Soul, the more aligned we are with our purpose and our Higher Will. As a result, the more natural it becomes for us to desire what is in alignment with our lessons and our Soul. When we get separated from our path, we struggle and suffer. It is very important to remember that learning does not have to be painful. Fill yourself with compassion and love for all those times when you struggled and suffered. Remind yourself that you can learn in peace and joy.

Sometimes we get used to the way we experience something and even become rigid about it. For example, many people celebrate certain holidays in a particular way. They become a ritual that needs to be performed in a specific way, according to our expectations, and if something changes, we might feel very uncomfortable. It seems like we can't enjoy change because it doesn't fit our rigid expectations; however, energy always moves and the only constant in life is inevitable change.

For example, for many years, a friend of mine would go to a restaurant and always order the same dish. One day, the restaurant removed the dish from the menu, and my friend felt very disappointed. She told me that she realized that if that tiny dose of rigidness could bring such disappointment, anything larger could be devastating. As a result, she decided to flow more.

Although "go with the flow" has become trivialized and almost cliché, it has a very powerful message. When we "go with the flow," we let go of rigid patterns and expectations. We have a clear idea of what we want, while we allow the Universe to bring it in the best way possible. It should not be done in a limited way we think is best. Remember that the Universe knows best, so make sure you do your work and let the Universe do its work

Finally, it is important to remember that when we are aligned with our Soul, the things that we desire and want to experience hold a lesson to help us evolve. For example, if we want to win the lottery, spiritually what we want is the essence of the experiences we could get by winning the lottery. It might be a sense of security, a feeling of peace of mind for having all your debts paid and your expenses covered, or a great feeling of abundance.

The clearer you are about what you want, the easier and the faster it manifests in your life. If you are clear about the essence of what you want to experience, the universe will find the best way to bring it to you. You can even "turbocharge" your intention by asking that the universe brings what you intend to manifest in Grace and for the highest good for you and all.

Communicate with your Soul so you have a clear idea of the essence of what you want, detach from rigid patterns, do your part and let the Universe do its job.

Go with the flow!

## WHAT TO REMEMBER

- Focus inward to understand what you want. Follow your heart and avoid setting goals that are not in alignment with your soul just to please others or because people expect you to do it.
- Meditation is a great way to get insights.
- We are the director of our life, co-creating reality by letting the universe know what we want.
- The highest outcome in our life experience is to evolve and become our Higher Self.
- Set your intention and then let the universe bring what you want in the best way possible.
- The clearer you are about what you want the easier and the faster it manifests.

# LET'S PLAY! – KNOW, FLOW AND ALLOW

Draw a flower pot or get the free download activity from my website.

- Write what you want on the pot
- Draw a dot in the center of the dirt and think about your intention
- Focus on your intention for ten seconds as you water your seed with light and love
- Draw a flower or a plant that comes out from the pot. The plant or flower is what you want to attract.

Congratulations! You have just brought the concept of what you want to this reality by drawing it. Use this drawing to visualize your goal in a tangible way!

When drawing for these activities, the goal is to enjoy the experience and process, so please do not struggle in order to make it look perfect. Draw as a little child that puts a dot of paint on a sheet of paper and then tells you a whole story about what she sees in the picture.

# VISUALIZE YOUR WAY TO SUCCESS

# ATTRACTOR STEP 2
# VISUALIZE YOUR WAY TO SUCCESS

*"The man who thinks he can and the man who
thinks he can't are both right."*
- Confucius

Our mind is a sophisticated lab and a marvelous art studio where our consciousness creates reality.

Several years ago, Andres and I wanted to move back to Austin, Texas, but because the housing market was doing so poorly, we were unable sell our house in Minnesota. During that time, Andres had just left his corporate job to start his own business, so we also knew that getting a mortgage would be difficult. We had some savings but the houses in Austin had already appreciated significantly, and the houses in the Hill Country were definitely out of our budget.

It seemed like an impossible endeavor but we were convinced that the idea of moving to Austin was best for our future. So the intention that we wanted to buy a house in the Hill Country was firmly set.

A couple of weeks later I had a dream where I saw myself in a house with windows that allowed lots of light to shine in. When I woke, I told my Andres that our house in Austin was already there, it was only a matter of waiting for it to appear. He must have thought that I was crazy but the very next day, I started visualizing myself in a particular neighborhood. Less than two weeks later when he went to drop one of our kids off to preschool, I decided to check the web for new houses in the market. I immediately found a new house on the market that was shortlisted with an unbelievable price. I called the agent that appeared on my screen right away. He, too, was shocked by the price, and when I heard how genuine his voice sounded, I told him I wanted to buy the house right away. This was likely more than he expected for a regular day of work.

"Don't you want to see the house first?" he asked. "Are you aware that you'd lose the deposit if you decide not to buy it?"

I knew this was the house of my dream and that I had to take quick action. I firmly replied that I was sure and that I would send the check right away.

Andres arrived a few minutes later and he almost fainted when I told him I had bought a house without seeing it and even worse, without talking about it together first. We visited the house some weeks later and it turned even more beautiful than we were expecting. It was full of light, right in the neighborhood that we wanted. It was priced so low since it was shortlisted but everything worked out miraculously. I learned later from my realtor that I had called just a few minutes after the house was placed in the market and that a few minutes after I called someone else called and tried to offer $10k more to get the house. I looked for the house at the precise time and knew I had to place the offer before Andres was back and that got us that amazing house and it all came to life because I committed myself to visualize.

Our thoughts have a very important role in the manifestation process. It is as if we are living in the sea of the All That Is, and when we focus on something and we start bringing it to our dimension just by thinking about it. We start giving it shape with our thought until it becomes matter.

Our mind is an amazing lab where we take the raw blocks of energy and translate them into 3D form.

I've always been amazed by the way the brain works and how we can change our life by shifting our thoughts. This is why I present you the biological effect of our thoughts and then I explain how to use our thoughts through visualization to manifest what we want.

## THE AMAZING MIND LAB

Our thoughts and feelings affect the way our brain works. We produce a type of nerve protein throughout our body and in our brain. These tiny pieces of protein are called neuropeptides.

Each emotion is associated with a specific neuropeptide. For example, endorphins are in charge of making us feel happy, serotonin is in charge of making us feel good, insulin is in charge of regulating our blood sugar and metabolism and so forth. These chemicals that flow throughout our body and brain are the same substances that are involved in emotions. This proves that there is a real body-mind connection and shows us that we can heal our emotional pain by altering our brain and body chemistry.

Every thought causes a chemical reaction in our brain that is transmitted as signals to our body. This then produces chemicals that make us feel exactly the way we are thinking.

Therefore, if we have happy, bright and positive thoughts, our brain produces neuropeptides that sustain those thoughts. This makes us feel happy, joyful, uplifted and inspired.

When we are looking forward to a trip, our brain starts making a chemical called dopamine. Dopamine turns our brain and body on, and we start feeling excited before we leave.

The body responds to our thoughts by having emotions. Our brain, which constantly monitors our body, will generate the chemicals to support those feelings, which in turn will promote similar thoughts. Sometimes, this cycle will eventually create a particular state in the body. Several studies have shown that our thoughts can change not only our brains but the cells and structures in our body. The placebo effect is an excellent example of the power of our thought.

Some researchers gathered college students, who were deeply in love, and showed them a picture of their loved one. Scientists measured the activity in their brains while looking at the picture. What they discovered was that just by seeing a picture, their brain would activate a section of their brains that would make them feel in love as if the person was with them.

Science has found that our thoughts and feelings have the power to switch our genes on or off. Thoughts produce chemicals that change our genetic activity. Therefore, our thoughts, feelings, and perceptions also regulate our biology.

You can shift your life by creating new neuronal networks and you can accomplish that by altering your brain and body's chemistry, which can be done by changing your feelings that are dependent on your thoughts.

## THE AMAZING POWER OF OUR THOUGHTS

The power of our thought is stronger than most of us realize. Quantum mechanics suggests that we all create our reality and that the observer influences the outcome.

You may know that when we're placing our attention on something, we influence the physical process of what we are observing. Thoughts create things or better yet, thoughts are things in an ethereal shape ready to materialize.

Since we know how powerful our thoughts are, it would be wise to use them to our advantage.

There was a design firm, with a large job to complete for a major corporation. This project would help the design firm to grow and distinguish itself from competition. Ultimately, this would result in higher salaries for everyone. They worked on the project for many days, with some employees staying the night. Eventually, the designers grew stressed and started to run out of ideas. Things were not going as expected, so the

33

director called all of the designers together for a meeting. He raised a glass half full of water. Some of them thought he was going to talk about the glass being half full or empty and how each of them would perceive it differently. Instead, the director started by asking – How much do you think this glass weighs? But no one could figure out where he was going with the question.

He continued by asking the same question again. Some threw out a random number, while others calculated the weight of the glass and then added it to the weight they calculated for the water.

There were many answers, ranging from 7 oz. to 16 oz. The director then continued, "It doesn't matter how many ounces or pounds something weighs, but how long you can hold it up. The numerical weight of the glass can be seemingly irrelevant if one can hold it up for a prolonged period of time. Stress and heavy emotions can put a huge weight on us, if we hold them for too long. This will happen if we allow our thoughts to focus on those things and feelings continuously. It will even get to a point where it will start to hurt, and we might feel paralyzed; however, if we acknowledge and release them, they will leave as quickly as they came."

Thoughts are like flowering plants or weeds. If we prune our plants and maintain the weeds at bay, we'll enjoy a beautiful flowering garden. By contrast, if we let the weeds grow wild, they can eventually invade our garden and kill the flowering plants.

We can let our thoughts run wild and kill the flowering happiness, peace, and joy, or we can take control of them and enjoy a happy, successful healthy life. The sooner we start, the faster we will start to enjoy the benefits and experience what is natural to us. This is what we now call miracles.

## HOW TO CREATE THE RIGHT THOUGHT CONCOCTION

From the very beginning, while in our mother's womb, we start accumulating experiences and stimuli. Even during the earliest years of our life, we are learning machines that store every experience in a hard drive, so to speak, called the subconscious.

Based on our experiences with the world and the experiences stored in our subconscious, we create beliefs that often rule our thoughts. Because our subconscious is so difficult to access, the challenge to change the information stored there is extremely challenging. That's why some behaviors or attitudes seem so ingrained within us. Think about it— there's information in our mind that we don't even know exists! So, it's no surprise that we remain stuck in the same patterns and energetic frequency, creating the same types of experiences, attracting the same type of people, and manifesting the same type of reality.

Hypnosis is a very effective way to change these patterns as the practice works directly with our subconscious. I am a firm believer in hypnosis and its benefits, but I am also a firm believer in providing people with the tools they need in order to make changes on their own. That tool is visualization.

Visualizing is creating a mental image or concept. We can create movies in our minds with the intention to manifest what we visualize. This involves using mental imagery to create what our heart desires. By creating a mental image or concept, we place our attention on the outcome we want. In this way, we start channeling the energy that creates this outcome into our physical reality.

The power of visualizing our desires is not new. For many centuries, "special people" would use visualization to create surprising results in the eyes of others. High-performance athletes, professional sports teams, and artists, for example, use visualization to accomplish their goals and to excel at the highest level of their field.

Our mind does not exactly distinguish between reality and imaginary. When we visualize, we are showing our mind what is possible. When we see movies or other people doing something, it changes our mental and even physical structure. For a long time, no one thought that it was possible to run a sub-4-minute mile. Once that record was broken, it then became easier for others to break it.

When we removed the training wheels from my oldest son's bicycle, it took him over a week to ride it confidently. Several years later, it took my youngest son, who had the visual example of two brothers riding without training wheels, about three seconds to do it. My dad held his back, so he could place his feet on the pedals, and off he went riding down the sidewalk. It was as natural as if he had been doing it for years. He knew what to do because he had seen it done over and over.

Studies have shown that when we visualize, changes take place in the body. For example, a study observed the brain patterns of weight lifters while lifting heavy weights. They then asked them to just imagine themselves lifting those weights without actually doing so, and they monitored the brain again. To their surprise, the same areas in the brain were activated while imagining as when they were actually lifting weights. The brain reacted the same way each time.

A research study performed by a sport psychologist at the Cleveland Clinic Foundation in Ohio showed the effect of visualization in our body. Guang Yue reported that "virtual training," or visualization, can increase muscle strength by up to 35%. Another study by Kai Miller at the University of Washington took this study even further, proving that "virtual exercise" or exercising using only our imagination, stimulates the same areas in our brain as when we physically exercise.

Many successful and famous people credit visualization as the strategy they use to acquire their success. Amazing personal stories about visualization have been shared by people, like Oprah Winfrey, Arnold Schwarzenegger, Will Smith as well as other top business leaders and athletes. It shows us that, as simple as it may seem, visualizing produces real and powerful results.

# HOW TO BOOST YOUR CREATIVE POWER

The goal of visualizing is to create an idea and to focus on it using your imagination. The idea must be given enough energy so that it can be manifested in the physical plane. It's a simple but powerful process. The only requirement is the will to do it.

Imagination is a key ingredient when visualizing. Many people associate imagination with a mental image, but there are different ways to use the imagination. Some people imagine things visually in their minds, while others can see actual colors when they use their imagination. And some people don't see an image at all when they imagine; instead they perceive the concept more abstractly. Every person has their own particular way to imagine and process information, whether through images, flavors, sounds, or textures.

We are all beautifully different, and even though I suggest techniques and steps to do or accomplish one thing or the other, please remember that there is no one recipe that fits everyone. Therefore, you should only do what resonates with your personal energy and feel free to adjust these suggestions to fit your uniqueness.

## THE VISUALIZATION MAXIMIZER MODEL

### KNOW WHAT YOU WANT

Clearly identify what you want. Take some time (minutes, days, or however long you need) to explore and decide what you truly want. Make sure it's what you want and not what your family expects of you or what your partner thinks would be better for you, nor what you think you must want, based on your current situation. For instance, someone while being strapped for cash might take a job that offers no growth.

Go within, listen to your soul, and choose what makes your heart sing. It doesn't matter how impossible or out of reach it may seem whatever it is that you want to manifest because the process of visualization indeed is to "bend" our reality, to make a shift.

So, sit quietly, focus your attention on your heart chakra (the center of your chest) and ask yourself what it is that you want to accomplish. Allow yourself to be bold and wild.

Our intelligence tells us what we need to do and tries to avert risk. We usually try to find the most natural path with the least effort. A perfect example is illustrated in the Pixar short film Inner Workings, a story about the internal struggle between the brain and the heart. The main character follows his intellect working in a job he doesn't enjoy. You can see that he would love to go out and meet other people and even eat ice cream, but the rigidness of his brain keeps him in that near miserable place. It is when he finally gives his heart a chance to guide him that he finds joy and love, exemplifying that we thrive when following our heart.

When we are willing to ask ourselves what our heart truly desires, we open ourselves up to the possibility of fulfilling our potential, as well as our mission on this planet. As a byproduct of this process, we often experience joy. Don't be shy! The sky is the limit (or maybe even beyond).

*Relax*

Take a few deep breaths, relax your body, and close your eyes.

Our brain works at different rates or frequencies throughout the day. Beta brainwaves are predominant while we are awake. It is a state where we are alert, engaged, and focused on cognitive tasks and the physical plane. When we are at Beta, we are rational. As I mentioned, we need to bypass our rationality to be able to focus on what we truly want without fear, attachment, guilt, or any negative emotion.

When we take some deep breaths and relax our bodies, our brain starts working on Alpha brainwaves, especially when we close our eyes. Alpha is a relaxed state of the mind. It is like when you are slipping into a daydream. This state heightens our imagination, learning, intuition, and, of course, our visualization process.

If you breathe and relax your body but notice that your left (logical) brain is still too active, you can count backward from 50 to 0. This technique will keep your analytical mind busy while you relax and prepare to visualize.

Relaxing not only feels good but is a very healthy state; therefore, make sure you give yourself some time during each day to enjoy this quiet and relaxing state.

# BE MINDFUL OF THE FOUR PS FORMULA

## PRESENT

Visualize your goal in the Present. Visualize it as if you have already accomplished it and as if it is part of your life now. See it, feel it, believe it, enjoy it! Remember that all possibilities already exist, you just need to focus on the one you want to bring into your life.

## PERSONAL

Make your goal personal. Focus on yourself. You are the focal point in your imagination, so perceive yourself having accomplished your goal. Remember the weightlifter example; if your brain processes you doing something in your imagination, it stores that information and opens the capabilities for success. This imagination process mimics the response in your brain as if you completed it in the actual physical world.

## POSITIVE

An interesting function of the brain is that it works optimally in positive mode.

If you present your brain with a negative concept, it may prevent your goal from being realized because of the perceived risk that accompanies negativity. For example, assume that someone says they want to lose weight. The subconscious might perceive just the losing side of the goal. As a result, it might not work toward that goal. Nobody likes to lose, right?

A better alternative would be: I am slim and fit or I have the power to adjust my weight in a healthy and beautiful way.

## PERSISTENT

When you focus your intention and work toward it every day, you begin to unleash your manifesting power. There might be challenges along the way when you are tired or just don't feel like you have time to visualize, but only three minutes per day will help you manifest your dreams better than if you spend three hours one day and then only continue two months later.

My friend Veronica had contemplated the idea of moving to Canada for many years but it was not until she visited her family a few months ago that she and her husband were determined to finally make the move. Moving to another country meant Veronica would lose her retirement; however, she was determined and open to allow the universe to provide a solution. She wanted to move with some financial security but didn't want to wait the many years needed to receive her retirement. Her will was so strong and in a very short time she met someone who mentioned to her that the company where she was working offered an early retirement for people, like Veronica, who had worked a required amount of years. She was so excited when she heard the news! She then designed a home screen for her phone with a picture from Canada and a text that said: "Good news! Thank you, thank you, thank you. I'm retired and moving to Canada." Her desires and expectations were so aligned with her visualization practice that it took less than three months for her to get her early retirement and move to Canada.

It's very important that you align your desires with your expectations because sometimes we simply wish for the best but expect the worse. Those negative thoughts create stronger ripples and the universe might give you what you expect.

You are capable of anything. Please remember that you have the choice to create unconsciously and let life happen to you, or you can be a deliberate co-creator with the universe and manifest the life that you want. Dare to dream big and expect the best.

## WHAT TO REMEMBER

- You can create an idea, focusing on it using your imagination and giving it enough energy, so it can be manifested in the physical plane. If you still feel unsure about this, try to envision an apple or banana and reward yourself when it appears in your life.
- The Visualization Maximizer Model: Know what you want; Relax; Four Ps: Create an inner image that is in the present in a positive, personal and persistent way.
- Every thought causes a chemical reaction in our brain is transmitted as signals to our body, which then produces chemicals that make us feel exactly the way we are thinking.
- Our thoughts program our cells and also change our genes.
- A fun, powerful, and easy way to train our thoughts and create the reality we want is through visualization.

- Thoughts are things in an ethereal shape ready to materialize, so be mindful of them.

## LET'S PLAY! – VISUALIZE YOUR WAY TO SUCCESS

Summarize something you want to attract in one or two words. Now imagine a symbol that represents what you want. It can be a feather, a crystal, a flower, or anything.

First draw a mountain, and then draw your symbol on top. Pretend that you are your pen or pencil and move it all the way to the top, drawing the path from the base of the mountain to its peak.

Remember that the goal is to have fun so please don't struggle to make it look perfect. Go with the flow, play with it, have fun. Use markers, crayons, paint or anything that you like, be creative!

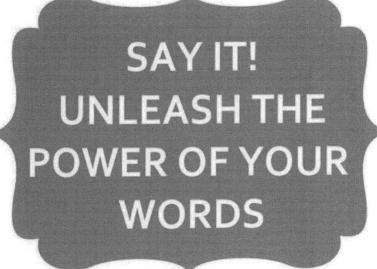

SAY IT!
UNLEASH THE
POWER OF YOUR
WORDS

ATTRACTOR STEP 3

# ATTRACTOR STEP 3
# SAY IT! UNLEASH THE POWER OF
# YOUR WORDS

*"If we understood the power of our thoughts, we would guard them more closely. If we understood the awesome power of our words, we would prefer silence to almost anything negative."*
-Betty Eadie

## IF YOUR WORDS WERE FOOD FOR YOUR SOUL, WOULD THEY NOURISH YOU?

Because of the way we experience our reality, we assume we live in a three-dimensional universe as three-dimensional beings. However, some scientists like Christof Koch and Sir Roger Penrose, among others, now propose that the entire Universe is consciousness, where nothing would exist without an observer. In other words, everything that we perceive and experience exists because there's some consciousness observing it, which means we create our reality by focusing our awareness on something.

While this is a fascinating hypothesis to consider, what we do know is that our words, thoughts, and feelings are codes that program our reality. Abracadabra!

How many times have we heard the word abracadabra without really knowing its true meaning? Many of us assume it's a word that magicians use to perform a magic trick. The true origin of "abracadabra" derives from Aramaic (the original language of the Bible) and means "with my word I create." In ancient times, it was such profound teaching that people would make a triangle with the word written three times. They would wear it around their neck so that they would remember the power of the spoken word.

Abracadabra is the magic we all have. It is the power to create with our words and the power to shape our reality, using them to tell stories that eventually become our reality.

As mentioned before, our brain doesn't distinguish between what we perceive first hand in reality and what we perceive with our imagination. This concept also applies to our words. Whatever we say, our brain starts working on those premises. Our words have a huge impact on the way we think and feel. For that reason, it is important that we consciously choose our words carefully. When we speak, we are gathering energy to manifest into our physical reality.

Words are energy and each of them carries a specific vibration. Positive words manifest positive realities. Words can be one of our best allies since they work as building blocks to create reality as we speak.

Some of us believe that our words reflect our life. In reality, it is the other way around. We are capable of shifting our life, by changing our words.

About a year ago, Lizbeth, a firm believer in the power of words and high vibe, wanted her son to attend a particular school. This school has such a good reputation that it had a two to a three-year waiting list, and admissions gave preference to families with siblings who were already enrolled, reducing her son's chance of being accepted even more. Eventually, Lizbeth got an interview with the school principal who revealed that her son did not meet the criteria for being admitted. Lizbeth requested that the principal grant a few months for Lizbeth's son to improve and meet the requirements. The principal felt it was a tough request to accept but agreed to give her the time. Lizbeth knew in her heart that this particular school was the best for her son. It was close to home and an excellent match for her son's personality. She hired a private tutor that would help her son meet the academic standards of the school while she committed to visualize and affirm that her son was admitted. It was not an easy job, especially since she was surrounded by naysayers telling her to apply to other schools as her son was not likely to be accepted. However, each time someone came with negative input, she would replace those comments with: "I'm grateful that my son is admitted to the school." She kept on repeating positive affirmations and feeling grateful. The deadline came, she met with the principal, and she was filled with joy and excitement when hearing the news. Against all the odds, her son was admitted to the school of her dreams.

## OPENING TO RECEIVE AND ALLOWING

In the previous chapter, I talked about the importance of intention when we want to attract something into our life. In addition, we must practice allowance and giving ourselves permission to be open and receptive.

Allowing yourself to open up to the gifts that the universe has ready for you is powerful and necessary. This is a free will reality, so if you don't give yourself permission to manifest and to attract what you want into your life, you just won't get it.

A simple way to allow yourself to succeed in manifesting is simply by saying it. You can say it out loud, say it quietly, or use words to say it in your mind's voice.

Here are some examples of what you can say to allow yourself to manifest. You can use these phrases or you can create your own. The idea is to open up to receiving and allowing.

"I am open to and give myself permission to co-create with the universe and succeed at manifesting."

"I allow myself to receive (state what you want) in grace and for the highest good."

The universe is constantly giving us that which we ask for with our words, thoughts, and feelings. Sometimes the simple act of giving yourself permission to attract what you want is all it takes to set the universe in motion and bring it to you.

## THE WVP MODEL (WORD VIBRATIONAL PRINCIPLE MODEL)

Words have a specific vibratory frequency as everything else in the universe. The WVP model is a simple way to understand the energetic effect of words in our reality.

*POSITIVE WORDS ARE CREATORS OF*
*POSITIVE REALITIES.*

As we use positive words, we are creating a higher vibration that will attract better outcomes.

*WHATEVER WE SPEAK CONSTANTLY,*
*WE CREATE REGULARLY*

Words are spoken thoughts and because thoughts are things, words have the power to accumulate the energy to create things that match their vibration. Positive words will create a positive reality.

*WORDS ATTRACT SITUATIONS AND EVENTS INTO OUR*
*LIVES, WHETHER WE SPEAK CONSCIOUSLY OR NOT*

It doesn't matter if you are running an old subconscious way of talking or if you are using affirmations and talking mindfully, either way, you are creating your reality through your words, so choose them wisely.

*WORDS, THOUGHTS, AND FEELINGS ARE INTER-*
*RELATED. MODIFYING OUR WORDS IS AN EASY WAY*
*TO SHIFT OUR THOUGHTS AND FEELINGS TO*
*CREATE THE REALITY WE WANT*

As I mentioned before, words are verbal thoughts and they have the power to train our inner thoughts to be more positive and focused so we can attract what we want.

*WORDS HAVE VIBRATIONAL PATTERNS THAT ARE
CAPABLE OF HARNESSING GREAT THINGS.*

As you choose your words mindfully you are creating a positive vibrational frequency that will help you attract a higher reality. The higher the frequency of your words, the better the reality that you can manifest.

*WORDS THAT WE SPEAK OUT LOUD CAN AFFECT HOW
ENERGY MOVES THROUGH SPACE AND FOR THAT
REASON CAN BE USED TO DIRECT ENERGY*

Sound is very powerful and can help tune whatever is around it to that frequency. You can use this effect consciously to surround yourself with a higher vibrational frequency and improve your manifestation power.

Words are the energy we are broadcasting out to the universe. When we speak, our words are transmitting the vibration of our thoughts into the universe, which answers by granting us that which matches the frequency we're broadcasting. By choosing our words carefully and wisely, we start painting the reality our heart wants to manifest. Since we are co-creators with the Universe, whatever we say goes; therefore, when we control our words, we have a conscious impact on our world.

By speaking words, we start solidifying thoughts. Thoughts have faster and lighter energy. When we convert them into words, the energy becomes slower, making it easier to materialize. This means we must choose our words wisely, using only those that work toward our highest good.

An easy way to practice choosing our words consciously is by using affirmations.

Using affirmations is a proven method for improving our life since they can purify our thoughts and rewire our brains.

Affirmation comes from the Latin word affirmare, which means "to consolidate, to strengthen, to make firm." Affirmations are words that consolidate or make our thoughts solid and stronger.

Positive affirmations have the ability to raise the level of our "feel good" hormones.

When we speak, our neurons also communicate. Neurons use an electrochemical cue to "talk" to each other and signal our adrenals to release specific hormones, such as dopamine (the "feel-good" hormone).

On the other hand, when there's no pathway between neurons, such as when we are learning or experiencing something new, those electrochemical signals are converted into neurotransmitters or molecules of emotion that help make new neuronal connections. This means that even when our brain structure seems to be fixed on a feeling or a way of thinking, by using specific words or affirmations we trigger a neurochemical reaction that can alter the structure of the brain to bring about change in our life.

The power of affirmations resides in its ability to program our mind, by making it believe what we are stating. Again, the mind has a hard time knowing the difference between what is real and what is fantasy. We can all create our affirmations, based on what we want to create.

A simple affirmation can change the course of things in a life. That was the case for Carolina.

I normally pay my employees through direct deposit but on this occasion she asked me to cut a check early as she needed to make some payments. I had the check prepared for her and decided to add a post-it note to show my appreciation for her work: "Carolina, abundance now and forever." She told me later that she loved the phrase and decided to use it as an affirmation constantly. To her surprise, she started finding money in the weirdest places and felt like she was becoming a money magnet all due to the use of a simple affirmation.

## 7 SIMPLE STEPS TO CREATE AN AFFIRMATION

### STEP 1: KNOW WHAT YOU WANT AND WRITE IT DOWN

Make a list of the things you want to change or manifest and write your affirmations.

### STEP 2: MAKE IT PERSONAL

Start with the words "I am" and make affirmations for you, not others.

### STEP 3: MAKE IT POSITIVE

Speak using the positive mode. Instead of saying, "I don't accept bad things into my life," say, "I am attracting amazing things into my life."

## STEP 4: MAKE IT SPECIFIC

Be as clear as you can and avoid ambiguities.

## STEP 5: MAKE IT BRIEF

Keep it simple and short.

## STEP 6: MAKE IT IN PRESENT TIME

Use verbs in the present tense.

## STEP 7: SAY IT OUT LOUD OFTEN WITH AWARENESS

Be conscious of all your words and repeat the affirmations you create consistently.

Make sure you are persistent when you use affirmations. I suggest that you start with one or two. Repeat it several times during the day, every day in a consistent way.

## 30 POWERFUL AFFIRMATIONS

HAPPINESS

I hold happy thoughts and attract blessings into my life.

My life is bright and happy.

I am kind, loving and happy.

FORGIVENESS

Let go and let God.

I am here and now living with compassion.

I forgive and forget.

HEALING

I am grateful for my health.

My body works in perfect balance.

Perfect health is my birthright and I embrace it now.

INSPIRATION

Doors of success and opportunity are always open for me.

I am a unique being of light capable of great things.

Life is beautiful and good.

Every day I manifest good in my life.

LOVE

I love myself and that state of love brings more love into my life.

I radiate pure, unconditional love.

My heart is open, I love, I am loved.

## PROSPERITY

The universe is abundant. I'm always provided for.

The universe always takes care of me.

I am abundant in all areas of my life.

I always attract prosperity, wherever I am and whatever I do.

## RELATIONSHIPS

I am surrounded by love. I find love in all relationships.

I am a good person and attract good people into my life.

The relationship with myself and others is always peaceful and harmonious.

## WHAT TO REMEMBER

- Our words, thoughts, and feelings are codes that program our reality.
- When we speak, our words are transmitting the vibration of our thoughts into the universe, which answers by granting us that which matches the frequency we're broadcasting.
- Choosing our words carefully and wisely is important to create the reality our heart wants to manifest.
- An easy way to practice choosing our words consciously is by using affirmations.

## LET'S PLAY! – SAY IT! UNLEASH THE POWER OF YOUR WORDS

If your words were food, what are you feeding your spirit?

1. Write what you want to feed your spirit. Love, joy, peace?
2. Draw lettuce or flowers and put each food for your soul inside one of them.
3. Affirm that you are open to receive all that.
4. Now charged with the good vibe of the "food" you gave to your spirit, create an affirmation to manifest that which you want to attract to your life. Write it on a different piece of paper and decorate it with markers paint, scrapbooking paper…

Just have fun, play with the activity and let your creativity flow. Don't struggle to make it look perfect, a sketch with a pen on a napkin will have the same results as a masterpiece on canvas when your intention and your energy are high.

# ATTRACTOR STEP 4

# RAISE THE BAR

# ATTRACTOR STEP 4
# RAISE THE BAR

We are like antennas broadcasting information all the time. The way we communicate our desires to the universe is through frequency. Our thoughts, words, and feelings of emotion all vibrate at their own particular wavelength or frequency. Using these frequencies is fundamental for attracting what we want to our life. And in that way, when our frequency is higher, we thrive in life, flow effortlessly and manifest easier and faster

Everything is made up of energy vibrating at different frequencies. This includes something that seems as solid as a rock to something as ethereal as a feeling.

A rock may seem solid and still; however, there are millions of subatomic particles within it that are moving around with energy. Therefore, the rock is pure energy in motion, vibrating at a rate that forms a particular wave and so we go down to a sub-atomic level, we no longer find matter but pure energy.

Frequency is the vibrational ratio that forms a wave, either in a material field (as in sound waves), or in an electromagnetic field (as in radio waves and light), usually measured per second.

Just like we can measure the frequency of sound or light, recent breakthroughs have allowed scientists, like Dr. Hawkins, to measure a person's energetic frequency on a particular scale.

According to Hawkins, we have a scale of 1 to 1000 with 1000 being the highest state a human can achieve—an Illuminated Master. On the lower side of the scale, would be someone who is languishing.

The most interesting thing is that humans on this planet vibrate at an average frequency of 200 on the Hawkins scale. What may seem odd or contradictory is that the collective human consciousness vibrates above 200. This is possible because some people vibrating much higher than 200 raise the bar. Those individuals counterbalance lower frequencies and raise the collective consciousness.

Heavy emotions like fear, sadness or guilt have a vibration under 200, while uplifting emotions like gratitude, love, and enlightenment vibrate above 200.

The higher your vibration, the higher your consciousness and vice versa. One person vibrating at a frequency of 500 can compensate for thousands of people vibrating at a lower frequency. Someone vibrating at a level of 700 can compensate for 70 million low vibrating people.

## THE MAHARISHI EFFECT

An example of how an individual's higher frequency can affect the collective consciousness is the Maharishi effect.

In the 1960s, Maharishi Mahesh Yogi described that a specific percentage of people (1%) practicing transcendental meditation could produce a measurable effect on the environment and the quality of the entire population. During the practice of transcendental meditation, the meditators enliven what Maharishis called the "unified field of natural law." When enough people activate this field, it starts radiating order and harmony, affecting the consciousness of the whole city.

In eleven US cities, between the mid-1970s and the mid-1980s, research scientists discovered that when the number of people participating in transcendental meditation reached 1% of the total population in a city, the crime rate decreased. This was an indication of increased harmony in the entire city.

We often have the belief that we can't do anything about what is happening on our planet or what is shown to us in the news, but every individual can make an important contribution by raising and maintaining their vibration.

Our emotions are closely linked to the frequency at which we vibrate. According to Dr. Hawkins, each emotion we feel has a vibrational impact on us, as shown:

| EMOTON | FREQUENCY |
|---|---|
| Enlightenment | 700 - 1000 |
| Peace | 600 |
| Joy | 540 |
| Love | 500 |
| Reason | 400 |
| Acceptance | 350 |
| Willingness | 310 |
| Neutrality | 250 |
| Courage | 200 |
| Pride | 175 |
| Anger | 150 |
| Desire | 125 |
| Fear | 100 |
| Grief | 75 |
| Apathy/Hatred | 50 |
| Guilt | 30 |
| Shame | 20 |

We are broadcasting waves of energy constantly and the higher our frequency, the easier and faster we manifest. It is very important to keep in mind that we contribute to the energy that helps others raise their vibration. By taking take care of your vibration and making an effort to consciously live at the frequency of love and beyond, we create a field that raises everyone's frequency around us, wherever we are and wherever we go. It is done simply by being there.

In my opinion, when we raise our frequency, we can absorb more light, until it gets to a point that we radiate that light to others without words or actions. It occurs just by being around them. The amazing aspect being that just by setting this example, we in turn set energy in motion for someone else to start raising their own frequency. That's the generosity of the Universe; we get the perks while effortlessly being a huge service to others.

As with everything we do and want to manifest, our intention is the first ingredient. Therefore, if you feel like doing so, set your intention to vibrate at a love frequency.

Raising our frequency should be easy. We were created to enjoy, thrive, be happy and abundant.

As you can see in the Dr. Hawkins' vibrational frequency of emotions chart, joy has a frequency above 500. This means that simply by finding things that bring us joy, we can raise our frequency.

Children are a gift to this planet. Because they are closer to Source, they vibrate at a higher frequency than most adults. They are in a state of wonder, enjoying every discovery. They are in a playful mode and mostly full of joy. I've taught art to kids for several years now. Every time I'm surrounded by them, no matter how busy the day or how tired I might be, their energy recharges me, fills my heart with joy, and makes me vibrate at a higher frequency than I was vibrating before. Children teach us that whatever fills our heart with joy, will raise our vibration effortlessly.

We all have had moments where we might feel down, feel funky or in a bad mood. That is natural to our human condition. When this happens, the first step to take is to acknowledge that state, allow yourself to feel that way and ask your body, mind, and spirit what they are wanting to communicate to you. Then as soon as you can, start raising your frequency again. What I mean is that when you experience a strong emotion like anger, don't try to bury it deep down. Simply release it quickly so you can get rid of it without involving others. You can write it down and then tear or burn the paper, go for a walk, write it on your computer and hit delete.

## THE GOOD VIBE RESOURCE LIST

Quick and simple ideas to boost your frequency.

### *BREATHE*

Sometimes all it takes to increase our vibration is to take several deep breaths. When we breathe deeply, we bring oxygen and universal energy to our lungs and cells. This helps us to raise our vibration.

### *GO OUT IN NATURE*

Trees and plants are great allies who do not only provide oxygen. Scientists have discovered that trees emit phytoncides, which are scents of volatile oils that help our body decrease blood pressure, blood sugar, and cortisol levels (cortisol is a "stress hormone"). Being in nature improves immunity, vitality, and creativity.

In Japan, for example, they use shinrin-yoku or forest therapy as standard preventative medicine. In this practice, people enter a forest intending to take a "forest shower." They sit in their preferred location for at least 20 minutes and mindfully observe all details of the forest including the smells, sounds, and color.

At an energetic level, plants absorb carbon dioxide and provide oxygen in return. They also absorb our lower energies and radiate a higher vibration that positively affects our energy field and easily helps raise our vibration.

*LAUGH*

Have you ever heard the phrase "laughter is the best medicine"? Besides making us feel so good, laughter lowers our blood pressure, reduces our stress level and boosts our immune system. When we laugh, our brain releases dopamine and this results in a calmer feeling. We then start smiling, which in turn, makes our body release endorphins (happy hormones). Before we know it, we feel joy. Laughter is like a mini-meditation to me. It is very healing and refreshing. It is a great tool to raise our frequency quickly.

*SING AND DANCE*

Music has a special effect on our vibration. It helps us to transform the discordant energy into higher vibration energy.

Because our DNA vibrates at a specific frequency, when we resonate with the energy of love, our whole being starts harmonizing. For instance, music recorded at 528 Hz is said to be the sound that resonates with the heart of creation and is a great way to raise our vibration.

Many studies have proven that music has a profound impact on us both physically and energetically. The Mozart effect proves how students perform better on tests and even cows give more milk just by listening to the composer's music. Levitin's study shows that music can have physiological effects since it releases chemicals as we listen.

Whether you dance to the rhythm, sing a favorite song, or just listen to a song, you can use music to raise your frequency. Just make sure that you listen to a melodic song, on with a positive message for your cells. Some songs might have a good rhythm, but the lyrics can bring someone's energy down. So be mindful about the music you play to raise the vibes. Music has a vibrational frequency that when it interacts with your energy field, affects it. You can use upbeat music to help you get back in the flow.

*GET MOVING*

Engaging in physical activity is a great way to move your energy. When we get our heart pumping oxygenated blood and our endorphins flowing in our body, we are also activating our aura and energy systems. Movement is great to raise our vibrational frequency.

There are many things that you can do to increase your vibration, besides the ones I just mentioned. This can include playing with kids or pets, breathing deeply several times, showering yourself with light (either mentally or physically), getting creative (painting, writing, creating music, coloring...), eating greens, playing with crystals or using essential oils.

Remember that whatever fills our heart with joy, will raise our vibration effortlessly. Very often the easiest practices get the best results.

## BLOW YOUR MAGIC CANDLE

A year ago, Andres and I went to Europe while my father stayed to take care of my children. We had everything planned to return a day before my birthday in order to spend it with my father and the children. After a wonderful trip, we headed to the Munich airport to return. Our flight had a connection in Canada, so we needed a temporary electronic visa. The visa is good for several months and I had traveled to Canada recently so I thought to use the one that had already been granted to me. To my surprise, it did not appear automatically when they scanned my passport. They asked me to try online with my phone, but the service was so slow that the page froze several times and I had to start over. Suddenly, the lady at the counter told us that there was no time to process the visa and that Andres had to board the flight immediately. I was stuck in Munich without a flight home.

I tried to take another flight but there was nothing immediately available and the flights the next day were exorbitantly expensive. Sadly, I began preparing to spend my birthday all alone and far away from home. I cried for about thirty minutes before realizing I had to consider this change of plans as an opportunity. It was actually a gift, right in front of me and I didn't see it at first! I looked for a flight to return as soon as possible and found one that departed two days later. The cost of that flight, including the hotel and the rental car, was even less than any of the other options. So I dried my tears and prepared to take advantage of the opportunity presented by the universe.

I bought a map and decided to drive to Innsbruck in Austria. The journey through the Alps raised my vibration significantly. I didn't spend my birthday as I was planning, but it was amazing nonetheless! It was a magical and most special trip. I got a great deal at an Innsbruck Hotel and everyone was super nice to me. I visited the Augsburg's Palace, ate my favorite food in front of the Golden Roof, and blew my birthday candle on a Strudel! On my way back through the Alps, my frequency was so high that I felt euphoric, so I took the opportunity that the universe gave me to manifest growth for one of my businesses. Less than a year after manifesting, I got new clients, and the business grew over 30% from the previous year. That made me so happy, and of course, I took the chance to "blow another candle," continuing a chain of magic candles.

It's those times when we are at a high frequency that things manifest easily and quickly. Here's a tip: Picture in your mind a time at a birthday when someone lights the candles, the birthday person focuses on a wish, inhales some air, and then blows out the candles excitedly. Imagine our "high-vibe" moments as if the universe is lighting a candle for us. We only need to focus our energy on what we want—much like a birthday wish—and release it with excitement to the universe.

So next time that you experience a "high-vibe" moment like when you feel very happy, excited or motivated, remember it's time to blow your candle and use that high vibrational energy to start manifesting something.

## WHAT TO REMEMBER

- Everything vibrates at a specific rate. This includes both "matter" and energy. When we go down on a sub-atomic level, we no longer find matter but pure energy.
- Our vibrational frequency communicates our desires to the universe and so it's fundamental for the manifestation process.
- The higher your frequency, the easier and faster you attract what you want to your life.
- The higher your vibration, the higher your consciousness and vice versa.
- Vibrating at a higher frequency is a great service that not only benefits us but the entire world. A very high-frequency person can compensate for thousands of people vibrating at a lower frequency.

## LET'S PLAY! – SAY IT! UNLEASH THE POWER OF YOUR WORDS

Think of a situation when you felt amazingly happy, successful, or just plain good. Remember how you felt and be grateful for that moment. Draw a symbol for that feeling. It can be something as simple as a heart or a circle but big enough to fit your name and a few lines. Write your name inside the symbol then hold that special feeling and focus on something you want to manifest. Write what you've focused on down inside your symbol.

Remember to have fun and draw as a little child, go with the flow. Be happy!

Use any materials that you have handy, or that motivates you. Markers, crayons, paint ... Remember that even a napkin and a pen will do.

# ATTRACTOR STEP 5

# MAKE SPACE FOR IT

# ATTRACTOR STEP 5
# MAKE SPACE FOR IT

When we want to attract something into our life, we first need to make space for it. This is when a decluttering process comes in very handy.

Decluttering is simply getting rid of what no longer serves you physically, mentally, emotionally or spiritually. You can declutter your room, house, office, relationships, health, your financial situation and so forth. Usually, when we have clutter in some area of our life—either physically or emotionally—it represents what we are allowing to obstruct the abundance flow.

Decluttering is letting go of that which is obstructing the flow so we can make space for something better, something new.

Sometimes we hold on to things waiting for something better to replace before letting go; however, the process should go the other way around. Imagine trying to get a coffee refill with a full cup. When we hold on to things, people or situations, out of fear that we might not get a better replacement, we're giving the universe the wrong message. Letting go sends the universe the message that we are certain we'll get something much better.

Several years ago, due to the recession, we had to move back in with my parents, since Andres had sold his business and couldn't find a job. This move opened up space for us to accept new things coming our way. During this time, I gave conferences on how to Overcome Stress through Meditation, on The Law of Attraction, and Self Hypnosis among others, while helping my dad with his business. The whole situation was tough for the entire family. After a couple of years, we bought a business for me to run and although it was a lot of work, it was a blessing because it allowed us to re-build our life. We were able to move back to our home and provide well for our kids. It allowed Andres to start his own business and land on his feet happily.

My passion has always been writing and teaching. I knew that if I wanted to pursue that passion, I would need to divert my attention from my beloved art business. However, I was reluctant because the business had been a "lifesaver." It was hard for me to let go of control, but I knew the time was overdue for me to do so.

One day when I was speaking on the phone with my mom, she recalled the man who found a canoe when everything around him was flooding. The canoe saved his life, so he decided to carry it around in case he ever faced another flood. It was heavy and made his journey tough and slow. One morning, he saw a bird flying freely. He decided to take the risk to leave the canoe behind and continue his journey. It was amazing! Everything seemed so light and easy. If he only had left his canoe many years ago, he thought, life would have been so much easier.

There are things, situations, and relationships in life that are like the canoe from my mother's story. We need to know when to hold on to it and when to let go.

We are all different and behave in different ways. For some people, painful experiences transform their lives for the worse. For others, it transforms their lives for the best. For some individuals, it might be easier to let go of the canoe, and for others, it might seem almost impossible. This reminds me of the story of the two sons.

There once was a man with two sons. The man was always drunk. He would spend all of his money on alcohol and would not provide anything for his family. The kids had a very good friend who would often have them over for something to eat. When they finished high school, they each moved to a different city far away from each other, thinking they would not see each other ever again.

The years passed and the good friend decided to seek out and visit the two brothers.

One of the brothers had just finished his master's degree and had a loving wife. He was an amazing dad with his two girls. He was very happy. His friend asked him how he had gotten to such a good point in life. He replied to his friend that after what he had lived through with his dad while growing up, he promised himself that he would forgive his father. This was because he was such a great example for him of what not to do. That was a great opportunity to learn how to be a loving husband and father who would provide for his family.

Then he went to visit the other brother. He was miserable, with barely enough money to survive. The little money he had, he would spend on alcohol. His friend asked him what had happened. He replied, "What else could you expect! After the bad example my father set, I couldn't be anywhere else but where I am now." The friend was a renowned psychologist who helped him learn to forgive. Several years later, he had a completely new and happy life.

Like the two brothers, two people can have the same experience. However, each of them might react completely differently. People relate to us, according to their framework. We also relate to others, according to our framework. For that reason, it can be hard to try to change others. It's important to remember that we have control over our reactions, our feelings, and our thoughts. From that standpoint, we can change the situation.

## THE ART OF LETTING GO

We attract people and circumstances, according to the lessons we need to learn. The outer world reflects our inner self. Things that we dislike or that are unresolved inside of us will be re-created in the stories that show up in our lives. For instance, if you had a boss who was rude and disrespectful, it would reveal that there are self-respect issues within you that you could address and heal and your boss in this case, was just the mirror of the lack of self-respect for yourself. Once that you worked on respecting and loving yourself, the issue with your boss would be transformed, either by not having that boss anymore or by a change in your boss attitude. When we heal the inner, the outer world transforms accordingly.

There's always a clue that tells us if we are in alignment or out of sync with our spirit. From situations to people, those cues are like a map that helps us navigate the sea of life.

Sometimes, the pain in our past traps us. As a result, we get stuck in the clutter of bad decisions, memories, betrayals, losses, guilt, injustices, etc. To be able to move forward, we need to let go and alter our perceptions and feelings to create a new reality to realize that we are not victims if we don't want to accept that paradigm.

The only thing that we have for sure in life is the ability to change; however, as intrinsic it is to life, we often resist it. This is because we are creatures of habit. Letting go means opening our hearts and minds to change and the possibility of transformation.

We can let go by becoming aware of our emotional barriers and confronting them, facing our fear, healing our guilt, and challenging our attachments to the past.

Letting go means going over a mountain and just keeping a pebble from our journey as a beautiful souvenir. We must leave room in the "backpack of our life" for something new.

Whether we are trying to let go of the judgments, a relationship, or the pain of the past, love and forgiveness powerfully helps us to lose attachments and to release fear and anger.

# FORGIVENESS

One of the common heavy loads that we carry with us is our grudges. When someone wrongs us, we feel justified in our resentment, anger, bitterness, and thoughts of revenge. It is common to carry those feelings around as a shield, so we don't get hurt again. But truthfully, behind the bitterness, anger, resentment or even feelings of extreme hatred, is the need for love.

As we carry around resentment and cling to those situations that have hurt us, we hold on to the past. This blocks the flow of love and deprives us of the gifts from the universe.

When we forgive, we let go of the grudge against the person that has hurt us. It liberates us from the "offended" role. When we are hurt, we are also more prone to hurt others. By contrast, when we forgive and let go, we lighten and brighten our path. By forgiving, we free ourselves from the heavy weight we have been carrying around. This allows us to start working miracles.

We are the most affected when we don't forgive. Whether we were wronged mildly or badly, when we hold the blame against someone else, we are prisoners of that situation. It is only when we let go, that we free ourselves.

Some of the most challenging experiences in life have to do with the heart. Who hasn't felt the heartache of losing a friend, a partner, a project, or a dream? Those situations are part of our lessons in this life. We have the choice of hardening our heart and building a fortress so we don't get hurt again, or we can let go, let God, and move on. If we decide to harden our heart and close it, we lose access to the light and the love that is readily available for us. We will likely encounter more situations and people who are reproducing exactly what we are trying to avoid.

On the other hand, when we choose to let go, we open ourselves to kindness and compassion. It is first for yourself and then for the others. We open our heart to grace and miracles so that we use our heart as it's meant to be used: to love.

We shouldn't forgive out of fear or obligation. It should be done as an act of profound love for ourselves.

Forgiveness isn't something we only do for others. We need to forgive ourselves first. We've all made mistakes and sometimes we are too hard on ourselves. Our ego, which is there to protect us, very often judges our actions harshly, making us feel guilty and disempowered. Keep in mind, though, that we widen our perspective and understanding when we realize that our soul is love and that everything else is an illusion until we release our grudges or negativity toward those situations and people of our past.

By forgiving, we release the anger and irritation. We also stop carrying pain as a reaction to someone's action. It doesn't mean that what happened is OK with us. It is a resolution to liberate ourselves from what's hurting, so that we become a vessel of love. Because love has a high vibration, it will shift our life rapidly in amazing ways.

Forgiveness can happen instantly, or it can take some time. However, it always starts the moment that we decide we want to release our disappointment, resentment, blame or anger.

## UNDERSTANDING AND COMPASSION

One of the key steps in forgiveness is understanding the "why". Why did I react in such a way or why did a certain person act that way? Was it out of fear of losing something or was it triggered by a childhood experience?

When we open ourselves to understanding, we start experiencing compassion.

Understanding breaks the ties that attach us to blame and opens the door for compassion, which allows us to forgive.

## EXPRESS YOUR FEELINGS AND LET GO

Sometimes old pain affects our present experience. If we have pain buried within from our childhood, for example, we can encounter situations and persons that will re-create whatever caused us pain. In order to heal this pain, we must acknowledge the past and how we might be re-creating these old situations in the present.

Therefore, if you feel pain, express it in a healthy way that offers relief. Revenge or making others pay for our pain only causes more pain and doesn't help us attract what we want. As we know, when we focus our attention on the negative, we bring back exactly that which we are trying to avoid or get rid of.

There are many other ways to release our painful feelings, such as writing a letter to the person. This will allow us to express all that we endured. Once we are done, we can burn the letter, or shred it and throw it away. This will allow us to release all the pain and the person or situation.

Another way to release painful feelings is to take a piece of paper and a pencil or pen and scribble or even break the paper with a pen. This will allow us to release one by one the feelings that we have been carrying around. This can be done with one or many sheets and over one or many days. Just make sure that each time you finish, you take a clean piece of paper. You should say, as I forgive I'm getting a clean slate. I deserve it and I'm thankful for it. You should then draw something that makes you feel good or just write a positive, uplifting word.

Changing your thoughts and your words is another effective way to transform your feelings and help you forgive. Words, like thoughts, have an amazing power to change our reality, as we'll see in the next chapter.

Forgive and give yourself a clean slate. You deserve it!

## JUDGMENT

Albert Einstein once said, "Everybody is a genius. But if you judge a fish by its ability to climb a tree, it will live its whole life believing that it is stupid."

Judging is a habit that, as a society, we have learned. Judging can start as a way of bonding. At other times, it starts when we feel scared to be different. It is a defense mechanism which makes us think that by putting others down, we might feel good or not isolated. We judge because we don't tolerate other people doing what we can't or because they are so similar, we just don't like it. We judge to justify our position and our point of view or to cover our insecurities and pain.

Whatever the reason for judging others, our judgments are ego strategies to avoid feeling uncomfortable.

When we judge, we are expressing that we feel wrong and there's also something wrong with others. However, there can't be anything wrong with us or with others, since everyone and everything is part of God, the universe or a creative force, existing at the perfect time and playing our role to grow and help others grow.

Judging usually hurts others. However, it always hurts us the most. Judging strikes back at us. Therefore, bringing others down or focusing on the negative, attracts similar energy back to our lives.

When we judge, we focus on an illusion. We place ourselves in a position of limited vision. Everything seen, and unseen is the Everything That Is, the Creator or Life Force. Everything is part of this perfection. When we judge, we are doing imperfect evaluations with a limited perspective. As we focus on the light within each of us, we widen our vision. Thus, we can see much more than we superficially see.

There's a story about a prince who was walking with his teacher on the street. His teacher was talking about the impact of thoughts and judgments on others. Therefore, he decided to provide an example. He said, "do you see that man on the street?" Could you think the worse of him?" The prince did as his teacher said. He had bad thoughts about the guy standing on the sidewalk and held those thoughts, as they passed by the man. A few minutes later, the teacher came back and asked the man, if he had noticed the guy he was with (the prince). "Of course, I did, he gave such a bad vibe and when he passed by, I felt so much hatred for him."

We all have preferences. That is what diversity means. However, a better way to express these differences is by discerning instead of judging. When we discern, we understand with compassion and acceptance, without an emotional reaction.

Discernment means to perceive how things are. Judgment is what we add after we discern. It is our will to make things the way we want. When we practice discernment, we understand with compassion other's behavior, even when we are not thrilled by it. We also open our awareness to understand our own beliefs and assumptions. In other words, we allow our heart to show us the teacher in the other person, as well as the lessons we can learn. As a result, each person we encounter becomes a true gift.

When we let go of judgment, we shed a heavy burden. We let go of a sense of dissatisfaction and stop the pain. We start appreciating more. We also learn to let go of the urge to control everything. This allows us to move forward wisely and in love.

When we let go of our blockages, like anger, resentment, sadness, bitterness, judgment or our past, we make room for new energy to enter fill that space in our life. By releasing, we make room for love, peace, hope, gratitude, joy, a new relationship or whatever our heart truly desires.

## A QUICK WAY TO LET GO OF ANYTHING

1. Get into a relaxed state.
2. Think of whatever you feel is blocking you and what you want to let go.
3. Locate the part of your body, where the block resides.
4. Call upon your Soul, your guides or your Angels.
5. Imagine yourself releasing that block from that part of your body and giving it to your Higher Self or your Angels. Therefore, it is taken to a place, where it can be transmuted into light.
6. Ask your Soul, your Guides or Angels to fill that space of your body with the purest light.

## WHAT TO REMEMBER

- As we carry around resentment and cling to those situations that have hurt us, we hold on to the past thus blocking the flow of love and the gifts that the universe has for us.
- By forgiving, we release the anger and irritation. We also stop carrying pain as a reaction to someone's action.

- Forgive and give yourself a clean slate.

- When we let go of our blocks like anger, resentment, sadness, bitterness, judgment or our past, we make room for new energy to come and fill that space in our life.

- Judgment is what we add after we discern. It is our will to make things the way we want. To heal judgement we can practice discernment, perceiving things from a neutral position, as they are.

- When we practice discernment, we understand with compassion other's behavior, even when we are not thrilled by it.

- Using discernment instead of judgment opens our heart to show us the teacher in the other person, as well as the lessons we can learn.

## LET'S PLAY! – MAKE SPACE FOR IT

Stress, fear, sense of lacking, guilt, and other lower feelings have a dense frequency that clutter our mind and our energy, making it difficult to manifest what we want. The practice of putting these things down on paper helps transfer the clutter out of your mind. For this section, draw four or more balloons. Inside each balloon write a thought or feeling that you feel has been cluttering your mind or energy. Imagine you let the balloons fly away and then toss the paper in the trash.

Have fun playing with this activity and letting your clutter go. Use colors, paint, or anything that you like. As in many things in life, it's the process that matters more than the final product, so enjoy every step.

# ATTRACTOR STEP 6

# ENERGY SELF-CARE

# ATTRACTOR STEP 6
# ENERGY SELF-CARE

Our thoughts are a form of energy that moves and interacts, not only at a physical level with our cells and DNA but also at an electromagnetic and vibrational level.

From an energetic angle, we are all made up of multiple vibrating layers that are beyond our physical senses. Each layer has a specific frequency and purpose; and they are interconnected to create an energy field around us that is known as our aura.

Our aura is an electromagnetic field that surrounds each of us, like an egg-shaped balloon of energy. If you go to an art museum, you'll find at least one piece of artwork that portrays a halo around the heads of highly spiritual people. Painting this halo or ray of energy was popular in, but not limited to, the ancient art of India, Tibet, China, and early Christianity. This halo is the aura that not only surrounds the head but our whole body.

The auras that surround us, are an electromagnetic field around our bodies. The "egg" formed by the aura expands from the body about two to three feet. Charismatic people often have much larger fields, while depressed or sick people have very contracted auras. However, it's important to know that the health and size of our aura, depends largely on the thoughts we think, the words we speak, the feelings we hold, and the way we act.

The aura consists of seven layers: physical, astral, lower, higher, spiritual, intuitional, and absolute planes. All of the layers are interconnected and each one has its own frequency. Our aura affects our thoughts, words, and feelings the same way that they are affected by our energy field. This includes our feelings, emotions, thought patterns, behavior and overall health. A state of imbalance in one of the aura layers impacts the balance of the others as well as the other energy systems of our being. When our aura is at a peak state, the rest of the energies encompassing the body are at an optimal balance, as well, and energy flows easily. If the energies of our aura are in harmony, then our energy centers are also synchronized and balanced. As a result, all of the energy systems within the body flow optimally, supporting our wellness.

## HARMONIZING OUR AURA

Making sure our aura is balanced and in harmony is a great way to manifest, change unwanted patterns, and to be healthy and happy.

The aura can hold the energy of fearful, unwanted, or self-destructive thoughts and block the natural energy flow. Drugs, whether they are prescribed or not, can affect the well-being of our aura the same way processed foods can.

Our environment also influences our aura. Therefore, the thoughts, words and feelings of others can have an impact on our energy. We often pick up other people's energies without being aware of it. Have you ever been in a good mood and all of a sudden, you feel angry or sad? At the end of the day, you might question yourself, not knowing what happened. This is a perfect example of how we are influenced by other's energies.

Many of us share this experience; however, the important question is, "How can I protect my aura?"

Each of us is responsible for our own personal energy and the care of our individual aura. I can't emphasize enough the power that our thoughts hold. They are the motor that moves our feelings and actions, thus impacting our energy field.

A healthy and strong aura ensures that life progresses smoothly, promotes better health, and attracts positive people and situations.

As we learn to cleanse and strengthen our aura, our energy levels increase, and we feel better.

## CLEANSING

In the same way that we take a shower to wash away impurities, to feel refreshed and clearheaded, cleansing our aura regularly is a great way of preventing negative energy to accumulate in our energy field and affect our physical body.

Cleansing our aura is the fastest way to boost our quality of life.

Cleansing your aura helps to clear your mind, body, and spirit of any blockages, stagnation or energetic disturbances that surround you, as well as the ones within you.

To cleanse your aura, you can use the power of visualization knowing that whatever you do in your mind is done for your energy.

### HOW TO CLEANSE YOUR AURA

Close your eyes and imagine your aura is a beautiful sphere of light that extends three feet from your body. Make it as beautiful as you can.

Then, visualize a beautiful waterfall of white light coming down from the sun. It permeates your aura and your body, filling your aura and all the cells of your body with light, washing away any discordant or stagnant energy, filling any gap or space with light and infusing your aura and your body with a beautiful vibration of love and light, leaving you energized. You can expand your aura to the size that feels comfortable, continue infusing it with light and when you are ready, open your eyes again.

### CLEANSING YOUR AURA WITH A SALT BATH

One of the easiest ways to clear and cleanse your energy system is to take a bath with sea salts. Simply pour three to four cups of sea salt and soak for twenty minutes.

There are many different techniques to cleanse the aura, like taking a salt bath or a simple shower. The key is the intention to release or wash away anything that is not for your highest good, so whatever ritual you choose, make sure it is with a strong intention to feel good and clear your aura.

Another alternative to this is using a sauna or sweat bath. Sauna means spirit, and it has been used for centuries by the Finish, the Russians, the Greeks, the pre-Hispanic Indians, the Irish and many other cultures as a way to purify the body, the spirit and the personal energy.

## STRENGTHENING YOUR AURA

Some people's energy is more sensitive than others. They instantly empathize with others, their energy systems are sensitive, and their energetic boundaries are somehow more open than other people. For these sensitive people, it can become overwhelming, since they are taking on and processing other's people energies, along with their own. We are all different and so are our energy systems, but across the board, we all benefit from strengthening our aura.

My favorite way to strengthen my aura is by raising my vibration. You can shield and protect your aura by visualizing a bubble of white or pink light surrounding you. That is a quick fix. Keep in mind, though, that when you raise your vibration, you attract the energy of a similar vibration and any lower vibration nearby will start vibrating at a higher frequency.

## A BOUQUET FOR YOUR AURA

There are some occasions where we are in crowded places and we want to delimitate our energy so that it doesn't get drained. For that purpose, we can imagine a beautiful bouquet of white flowers with very short stems that move around our aura, keeping it free from any drainage.

"Schumann Resonance" is an natural Earth field. It oscillates at 7.83 Hz. This is a frequency where our body flourishes and our energy centers move naturally into a state of harmony and balance. Just by taking a walk out in nature, we harmonize our aura and energy system.

## GROUNDING

Connecting ourselves to the Earth gives us a feeling of safety and protection, as we connect with our mother earth.

To ground yourself, go outside barefoot with the intention of connecting with Earth, feeling the connection of your feet on the ground. Another way is to imagine a golden cord that goes straight down your back until it reaches the end of your spine. Imagine it continues out of your body down into the ground until it reaches the center of the planet, which you might visualize as a sphere of light. Anchor your cord to the sphere of light. Let the light of the center of the Earth go up through your cord and fill your whole body. Any discordant and unwanted energy can also be sent to the center of the planet so that it's transmuted.

Because our aura holds patterns from the past, present, and future, we can manifest a wonderful reality by changing these patterns. By cleansing, releasing and being aware, we can move beyond our limitations.

Another simple practice is to imagine your aura as a beautiful sphere of light that extends three feet from your body. Make it as beautiful as you can! Then bring a shower of light on to it and imagine how the light washes away anything that is not in the interest of your highest good.

## THE CHAKRAS

Chakras are the centers in each of us where energy is gathered and transformed.

These amazing centers are energy vortexes of light, gateways of energy, or exchange points, where vital life force enters and the lower vibration energy is released.

Each chakra is correlated with a specific function, level of consciousness, and stage of development.

The most popular are the seven primary chakras aligned in a column called the Hara line. They follow from the base of the spine to the top of the head, increasing in frequency from bottom to top, each radiating a different color.

### THE CHAKRA SYSTEM

Although I'll explain each chakra separately, the chakra system is interactive. When a chakra evolves, all chakras transform simultaneously so that growth can take place harmoniously.

Chakras thrive and expand in the presence of love and light and can become blocked by fear.

On the other hand, chakras can be balanced and overactive or underactive. The optimal situation is to have open and balanced chakras. Although we have more than seven chakras, I'll focus on the seven most popular chakras located in our body.

## 1ST – ROOT CHAKRA

It is located at the base of the spine. It is red and relates to our survival and our desire to live in a physical world. It connects you to your culture, country and your "tribe." This chakra has to do with security, nourishment, and financial, medical, and shelter affairs.

Its function is to create health, wealth and security while promoting a balanced and fulfilling life.

If it's unbalanced by fear of not having enough to survive, people might feel blocked, unmotivated, physically tired, and powerless.

## 2ND – SACRAL CHAKRA

This chakra is located above the pubic bone and beneath the navel. It is orange and relates to the creative impulse, including reproduction.

Its function is to express ourselves creatively, to have healthy sexual relationships, and to be a valuable member of our family and community. If it's unbalanced by fear of losing control of your life and/or fear of being neglected or abused, people might feel detached, rigid, unable to cope with life's challenges and insecure. This can contribute to getting involved in unhealthy or abusive relationships.

### 3RD – SOLAR PLEXUS CHAKRA

It is located in the stomach area, right below the sternum (chest bone). It is yellow and relates to our identity, personal power, and ego.

Its function helps us decide what we want, our plans, and to manifest our dreams.

If it's unbalanced by fear of a lack of power, people might express excessive control over people and life or have a feeling of helplessness and irresponsibility. They can also experience a lack of clear direction and ambition, as well as having difficulty manifesting our plans and putting ideas into reality.

### 4TH – HEART CHAKRA

The heart chakra is located in the center of the chest. It is green and relates to love, compassion, harmony, and beauty. It is the chakra that integrates all of the chakras and the connection between body mind and soul.

Its function is to love yourself and others and to forgive, appreciate, transform and connect us.

If it's unbalanced, people might experience codependency, jealousy, difficulty to forgive, or difficulty to be pleased.

## 5TH – THROAT CHAKRA

This chakra is located at the center of the neck and throat. It is blue and relates to communication (speaking and listening).

Its function is to help us speak our truth, listen to our inner voice and align with the divine.

When this chakra is unbalanced, people may experience poor communication. They may be overly quiet or talk too much, without listening either to others or to their inner voice.

## 6TH – THIRD EYE CHAKRA

It is located between the eyebrows on the forehead. This chakra is violet and it's our intuition hub.

Its function is to help us perceive extrasensory information, inspiration, and to give us vision and intuition.

When unbalanced, we may have a hard time distinguishing what is real or feel as though we don't have a vision for our life, lack focus, judgment, and be unable to look beyond our current situation.

## 7TH – CROWN CHAKRA

This chakra is located at the top of our head and it's white.

Its function is to connect us with our Soul and our creator. It provides us with access to higher states of consciousness.

When unbalanced, we may feel disconnected to our spirit and be cynical about sacred and spiritual matters. On the opposite spectrum, we may disconnect from our body, which can be manifested as a physical ailment.

Keeping our chakras in harmony and balance helps us attract better situations and opportunities to manifest what our heart desires.

## HOW TO HARMONIZE AND BALANCE OUR CHAKRAS

There are many ways to harmonize and balance our chakras. The first step is to realize that we are in control of our energy and the systems of our chakras.

As a society, we have been trained to give away our power. We give away our power to heal when we affirm that only a doctor or a certain medicine can heal us. We give away our power to manifest when we believe that things are set and there's nothing we can do about it. We give away our power to create when we blame others for what we are experiencing.

We are beings of light capable of healing, manifesting, and creating. The outer world is a reflection of our inner world and works as a map to show us the way. If we feel discomfort in a specific situation in our outer world, we can look inward. This will allow us to understand discomforting situations are in our life to help us heal, so that inner "hole" can be filled with light.

At some point in my life, I used to feel like I had too many things to do. I would go from getting kids ready for school in the morning, running my business, doing household chores,

101

preparing dinner, and giving time to my kids and Andres. As a result, by 11 pm, I was exhausted and frustrated for not having had any time for myself. I would end up going to bed at midnight and would be tired the next morning.

I realized the lack of time for myself was a reflection of how I didn't make giving myself time an important priority. That was the moment when I decided to take care of myself first so that I could then take care of everyone else. Setting limits and giving myself time to read or simply go for a walk, bringing a huge change to my outer world. As I started giving myself time to enjoy life, the rest of the environment started opening. I noticed that I was having more free time to do the things I enjoyed.

We have the power to heal and thrive when we open and balance our chakras, and when we harmonize our energy, we maximize this power. There are many ways to help us balance our chakras: like meditation, visualizing them open and bright, chakra tuning forks, and a pure intention to balance the chakras can be a strong force that starts moving the energy.

Harmonious sounds and music can have a significant effect on balancing our chakras. Each chakra vibrates at a particular frequency. A sound that matches the optimal chakra vibration can open and balance that specific chakra.

Mantras or affirmations can also harmonize our chakras and allows us to clear energetic pathways, creating positive change in different areas of our life, from the spiritual, mental, and physical levels.

These are some mantras that you can repeat out loud to balance your chakras:

Root Chakra "Lam"

Sacral Chakra "Vam"

Solar Plexus Chakra "Ram"

Heart Chakra "Yam"

Throat Chakra "Ham"

Third Eye Chakra "Om"

Crown Chakra "Ah or Om"

These are more mantras that you can repeat out loud to balance your chakras (you can also come up with your own):

Root Chakra "I'm grounded, strong and provided for"

Sacral Chakra "I'm a powerful co-creator with the universe" "Creativity flows through me"

Solar Plexus Chakra "I accept and love myself completely"

Heart Chakra "I love myself and my life as well as everything and everyone that is part of it"

Throat Chakra "I express myself freely and accept other's expressions with love"

Third Eye Chakra "I'm open to perceive and receive wisdom and light"

Crown Chakra "I'm one with all"

**The Seven Chakras**

## WHAT TO REMEMBER

- The chakras are part of our energy system. These amazing centers are energy vortexes of light, gateways of energy or exchange points.
- We have the power to heal and thrive. In the same way, we can balance and harmonize our chakras and our energy.
- Mantras or affirmations can harmonize our chakras.

- Our thoughts are a form of energy that moves and interacts, not only at a physical level with our cells and DNA but also at an electromagnetic and vibrational level. To maintain optimum wellness, our physical body needs a vital energy force to flow in and around us. It needs our energy centers to be open and in balance so that our energy field is at its optimum state.

- From a physical perspective, our body is formed by an energy that vibrates slowly and, therefore, seems solid to our eyes.

- A healthy and strong aura ensures that life progresses smoothly, promotes better health and the attraction of positive people and situations. Therefore, harmonizing and cleansing our aura is a positive habit.

## LET'S PLAY! – ENERGY SELF-CARE

Imagine your aura like a shimmering sphere around you. Draw a smiling stick cartoon that represents you and a beautiful circle that represents your aura. As you draw, think or say good things about your aura like, "My aura is healthy and wealthy," or, "My aura is filled with light."

Relax and let your creativity flow. However your stick cartoon looks like, it's perfect, love it, enjoy the process of creating art your way! Very often my stick cartoon characters make me laugh out loud. So have fun with yours get your funny side out!

You can download the free play sheets and meditations created to go along with this book. Just email me at GertrudeMarie.gm@gmail.com

# ATTRACTOR STEP 7

# CLEAR RESISTANCE: TRUST THE PROCESS AND EXPECT THE BEST

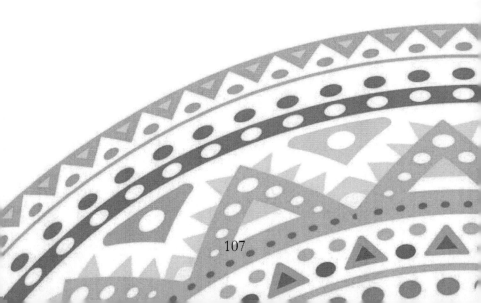

# ATTRACTOR STEP 7
# CLEAR RESISTANCE: TRUST THE
# PROCESS AND EXPECT THE BEST

Energy is the force that composes, unites, moves, changes and makes the universe flow. It's the potential to create change.

Because energy is the fundamental ingredient to manifest, I decided to dedicate this section to explain what energy is and how it works. Understanding energy is a very important step in attracting what we want for our life and fulfilling our purpose.

Energy cannot be destroyed or created. Energy can only change from one form to another. Everything that we see and perceive, as well as everything we don't see or perceive, is energy.

$$E = MC2$$

Einstein's famous equation means that energy and matter are the same, and that the only difference between matter and energy is the speed at which they vibrate.

*EVERYTHING IS COMPOSED OF ENERGY*

Whether it is light as a thought or dense as a rock, everything is energy. Nothing is excluded. Even our beliefs, expectations, thoughts, and words contain energy.

## ENERGY AND MATTER ARE CONSTANTLY EXCHANGING

Energy and matter are an intertwined, everchanging collaboration; therefore, whatever affects one, alters the other. When we visualize, we are working at an energy level. We are moving energy that affects our physical reality.

### ENERGY IS INTERACTIVE AND DYNAMIC

The nature of energy is to move and to interconnect. Moving energy fosters and preserves life, while stagnant energy creates blocks and an unhealthy environment.

Energy cannot be destroyed, only changed or transferred. It can be held in different patterns and with different intentions. In my opinion, energy can't be negative or positive. It can only be. If someone has a negative intention against something or someone, it would be labeled as "negative energy." This is energy that might flow backward or become sluggish and produce limitation. However, when the pattern changes, the purpose is met or the sender is enlightened. The energy that is released is just energy. It is neither positive nor negative.

We hold the belief that nothing is faster than light, but scientists have now discovered that light might not be the type of energy that travels fastest. Now we're learning that quantum entanglement moves faster than light.

According to quantum mechanics, when there are two electrons close together, they can vibrate in unison. They communicate information by sharing a frequency. When those same electrons get separated, they still vibrate in unison. This occurs regardless of how far apart they are. Even when they are on the other side of the world, information is still being sent and received instantly.

The universal consciousness operates outside space and time. Since we are connected to this consciousness, our thoughts operate in the same way. They are energy that can move at a speed faster than light.

There are a hundred trillion atoms in a cell and about the same number of cells in a human being. Each atom can have one or many electrons. This means our body has many electrons. I am sure that they have been entangled with other electrons outside our body and even outside our planet. That is one way that the universe works with us when we have a thought.

When we create from an ethereal energy point of view, we create in a faster and easier way. I call this way of creating energy, energy work. I like to do energy work first, before doing any physical work because it reduces the time and amount of effort that I need to put into any project.

When we do energy work, our cells start vibrating at the frequency of our thoughts. Since everything is alive with energy and the universe is responsive, our environment starts responding to that frequency.

Any thought—whether conscious, subconscious, of a high or a lower vibration—moves energy to manifest something that matches its frequency. For example, lifting a 50 lb. rock in our mind is much easier than what it would be on the physical plane. This is because thought is a lighter form of energy.

When we learn how to work with energy, creating first from within and then from without, we explore new possibilities where everything feels lighter and brighter. Tasks and projects become simplified and easier to manifest in the physical plane.

We can do energy work in any situation. For example, one of my clients was looking for a job and wanted some advice on how to find one. I told her that it was important to first know all of the details she wanted for her ideal job. This could include: being able to spend time with her family, earning X amount of money that would allow her to travel, etc. She made a comprehensive list, and then we started doing energy work. She created a symbol that represented all of the qualities she was looking for in a new job. Once she had that symbol, she imagined a beautiful light sphere. She put the symbol inside the sphere and sent it to the universe where it could gather the energy to manifest for her.

Within a month, she found an ad for a position that met all the criteria she was looking for. She sent her resume to the company, and they quickly responded with an interview request. She did her energy work again before the interview. She visualized the interview process and practiced speaking from her heart about how she could contribute to the company and how it would be her ideal job. When the actual interview took place, it seemed like the interviewer already knew her capabilities and what she was looking for. She had done the energy work beforehand and, therefore, the communication went very smoothly.

You can do energy work to eliminate obstacles, to speed things up, to open possibilities, to start your day, to attract money, and to manifest anything into your life.

Doing energy work is simply connecting with your soul, focusing, and becoming more conscious. Using your imagination and focusing your mind through images, symbols, or other elements is a fun and powerful way to play with energy and to create something on the physical plane.

An easy way to do energy work is by using symbols as it's easier to imagine something that represents what we want to manifest rather than a complex image. For example, if we are working on a project and all of a sudden we feel blocked, we can create an image that represents the blockage in our imagination. Then we can transform that symbol into something that releases the blockage. For example, we can imagine a wall in front of us and then convert that wall into a beautiful waterfall of ideas and light.

Adding light to our energy work can accelerate our manifestation process.

Light vibrates at a high frequency, so when you add it to your energy work, you are also raising your vibration, thus, speeding up the attraction process for whatever you want to manifest. In fact, your spirit and body are working with light all the time.

Light is a natural part of our life, and we all know how to link with it intuitively.

Just by thinking of light, you immediately draw it toward you and to that which you want to manifest.

Energy work with light is one of my favorite techniques for transformation because it works softly and smoothly while being very powerful. It only takes an intention to surround yourself, a situation, or a person, with light. The more we work with light, the easier it becomes to perceive and use in everyday, which will ultimately lead to amazing results.

## MANIFESTING IN THE NOW

According to the Chaos Theory, particles move in a seemingly random way but in a circular pattern around a specific point called the attractor. The stronger the attractor, the more definite the pattern of the particles and the closer they move around the center. Think of our consciousness as the attractor, so the more we are aware and focused on something, the faster and easier we attract it.

Time is eternal and multi-dimensional. Everything is happening at once. However, our consciousness is in the now, therefore it is of the utmost importance to take advantage of the amazing power of the now. Remember that the present is a gift. It's hard to manifest when your energy is all scattered in the past or the future. When you focus on the present moment, you're working with a stronger energy and intention. When we tap into our present, we reap many gifts, such as the Spirit.

When we focus our awareness on that connection, it is like we're re-calibrating our body, mind, energy and our whole self to the original specifications. It is no wonder why this practice can reduce our blood pressure, stress, and anxiety. It can also increase our tolerance, as well as our resilience and understanding.

Being in the present moment helps us enjoy more and suffer less. When we are in the now, it doesn't matter what is going on in our life, what we have accomplished, what has happened in the past, or how much money we have.

A fast and easy way to be in the present is to breathe.

Breathing is not only related to our body. When we breathe, our mind calms down and our emotions are balanced, allowing us to be in the now.

Many cultures throughout history have used the word Spirit and breath interchangeably. This is because, through breath, we connect to Spirit. My 4-8-8-4 METHOD is a simple way to practice focusing on our breath.

### 4-8-8-4 METHOD

Begin by putting yourself in comfortable position with a straight back and your arms and legs uncrossed.

- Breathe in quietly and slowly through the nose for a count of 4, letting the air go all the way to your lower abdomen.
- Hold your breath for 8 seconds

- Exhale through your mouth with a whoosh sound, for 8 seconds.
- Repeat the cycle up 4 times.

## THE PRESENT OF MEDITATION

Another way to be in the now is through meditation.

Meditation involves focusing our awareness on a specific point, but although it's not its primary goal, meditation supercharges our manifestation process.

Mediation is about training our awareness and connecting with our Source. By connecting with All That Is, we open up to our highest qualities like peace, joy, love, and many other high-frequency energies. It's "emptying our cup," so the universe can pour the finest coffee into it.

Many people have the idea that meditation is about turning off our thoughts or feelings, but meditation is about acknowledging our thoughts and observing our feelings without judging them. Meditation puts you in the driver seat of your mind.

There's a vast number of articles and studies that prove the amazing benefits of meditation, like improving health, self-discipline, performance, emotional healing, finding peace, and getting clarity.

Sometimes it is hard to get clarity about what we want. People often ask me how we can gain clarity and find focus, and my answer is meditation. Lacking clarity often comes from allowing our thoughts to clutter our mind, and allowing the noise of the outside world to block the sound of our spirit. When we meditate, we reconnect with our Soul, we become conscious of who we really are, and at this level of consciousness, there will always be clarity.

The last time I was in Austria, I tried an apricot cake that I loved, so I got the recipe for it. Back home, I bought all the ingredients and with excitement started mixing everything in the amounts and order following every detail of the recipe. The batter looked perfect, and I had set the oven at the required temperature. It was then when I realized that my son had made brownies the night before and had left them in the tray I needed for the cake. I needed to be quick, and I didn't want the batter to get ruined, so I took out a plate and started transferring the brownies as fast as I could, but there was a portion stuck to the tray. I began feeling stressed and worried. Sponge and soap were not enough, so I poured some hot water over the tray, let it sit for a minute and then removed all the brownie residue from the tray. Finally, the tray was clean and empty, ready to receive the delicious batter I had prepared. In our daily life, we are the tray. We process all sorts of "batters," but often end up with some residue that can clutter our mind just like the brownies that were stuck to the tray. You can't take a new "batter" even if it's delicious because it's full of crumbles and brownies. Meditation is like pouring hot water and waiting for a minute. It removes the residue from our mind leaving it clear and aligned to our highest qualities. When we meditate, we connect with our Source; thus, we elevate our energetic frequency significantly. And as we've seen before, the higher our vibratory rate, the more good we attract to our life including health, wealth, and everything in between.

## THE MANIFESTATION PRIMER

The time after meditation is what I call a manifestation primer because it sets all the necessary conditions to attract what you want to your life. Just think about it for a minute. As you meditate, you are "emptying your cup," clearing your mind and balancing your emotions, while raising the rate at which your energy vibrates. You are basically making space for what you want to attract while your high vibe is acting as a magnet to draw it to your life easier and faster. The brain waves after meditation are at the ideal level to program the subconscious mind. All these factors make the time right after meditation a very fertile soil to plant your intention seeds.

When I'm working on manifesting something, I include some additional steps to my meditation. First, I ask my Soul to embody me fully. Then quietly from my heart, I communicate my desire to align with my Higher Purpose and then imagine a bright light above me radiating my Higher Purpose onto me. I breathe in deeply several times imagining I'm absorbing more and more light with each breath. And then, following theses breaths, I begin meditating. Following my session, I release out to the universe that which I want to manifest.

If you are new to meditation, you can start by focusing on your breath, like in the meditation breath exercise. Another way to do it is to focus on an image, word or mantra or simply your body sensations. This will allow you to turn your attention away from our thoughts. When we meditate, we are in the now. We are not thinking about our to-do list or what we could have done better in the past. We are in the present, just being.

There are many different practices of meditation, like guided meditation, transcendental meditation, mindfulness, and movement meditation among many others.

In my experience with groups and clients, it's often easier to start with guided meditations to train your mind to focus on something and then move on to a more abstract type of meditation.

However, regardless of the type of meditation practice you choose, meditation has many advantages. Committing time to meditate daily, has benefits that have been scientifically proven including improving our physical, mental, emotional and spiritual health.

On my website gertrudemarie.com, you can find meditations to start or add to your meditation routine.

When we don't take time to "smell the flowers, we slow the flow of the abundant energy from the universe. It is when we practice being in the present moment regularly, that we keep that connection "clean", allowing the universal energy to flow in our lives.

## MEDITATION BREATH

1. Sit in a chair or on the floor. Make sure that you are comfortable, your back is straight, and your hands are either palm up or down on your knees or your lap.
2. Close your eyes and relax your body.
3. Inhale and exhale through your nose three times, feeling the air coming through your nostrils and filling your lungs.
4. Keep on breathing, focusing your attention on your nose and on the area where the air first touches your nose.
5. Maintain your awareness on your nose, while you continue breathing, letting the airflow in and out of your body.
6. Start doing this for five minutes. You can increase the time with practice.

## CREATING A NEW REALITY READING MEDITATION

This is a reading meditation.

As you read it silently or aloud, feel the words and imagine that which you want to manifest.

Sit comfortably and relax.

I put myself in a comfortable position with my back straight.
I take a deep breath, and as I do so, I bring light into my body and my cells.
I exhale slowly.
I release to the universe any situation, concern or energy that doesn't serve
my highest good.

I bathe my emotions and my thoughts with light

I grow calmer as I keep breathing deeply.

I allow myself to relax deeply.

I ask my soul to embody me.

I bathe myself with the purest light.

I align my body, my mind, and my feelings with my Divine Purpose.

I fill my heart with gratitude.

I fill myself with forgiveness.

I fill myself with love.

I allow happiness to fill my heart.

I am love.

I am in peace.

I am happy.

I bathe my thoughts and emotions with light from the Higher Planes.

I love all my thoughts.

I love all my feelings.

As I love my thoughts and feelings, they vibrate higher and bring about a better reality.

I love myself; I love my thoughts; I love my feelings.

I allow all my thoughts and feelings to flow, and I replace lower vibration ones with love. My thoughts and feelings grow more positive.

My frequency elevates.

My thoughts and feelings create a beautiful reality.

I imagine what I want to attract to my life.

I fill this idea with light.

I co-create this reality with the universe.

I am grateful because it has been given to me.

I feel joyful and excited to receive what I want or something better in the perfect form, time, and place.

I let go of any attachment and allow the universe to bring it to me in grace and the best way possible.

I am grateful

I am joyful

I am love

I am light

## WHAT TO REMEMBER

- Energy cannot be destroyed or created, only transferred or transformed.

- Energy can only change from one form to another. Everything that we see and perceive, as well as everything we don't see or perceive, is energy.

- Einstein's famous equation means that energy and matter are the same and that the only difference between matter and energy is the speed at which they vibrate.

- The more we work with light the easier it is to live in balance.

- Doing energy work before doing physical work takes the "heavy lifting" away.

- The present is a gift.

- A fast and easy way to be in the present is through breathing consciously.

- When we meditate, we are in the now.

- Being in the present moment, helps us enjoy more and suffer less.

## LET'S PLAY! – CLEAR RESISTANCE: TRUST THE PROCESS AND EXPECT THE BEST

Draw a circle and write your name in it. Above the circle, draw a sun with as many rays as you like shooting toward your circle. Write things you want to manifest over each ray knowing that the universe is sending you each of these things surrounded by light.

Remember, have fun, don't struggle to make it look perfect. Unleash your creativity and enjoy the process. Use whatever materials you have at hand.

# PUTTING IT
# ALL TOGETHER

# PUTTING IT ALL TOGETHER

## ATTRACTOR STEP 1
## DECIDE

Decide on what you want to attract to your life and set an intention. (Remember to add this to your intention: "In grace and for my highest good and the highest good of all.) Ideally, write it down and open yourself to the endless number of possible ways in which the universe can bring it to you. Keep in mind that because you are asking for it in grace and for your highest good, it will come in divine time, so detach and don't try to force the timing. Beware of strangling the energy it needs to manifest by forcing things too quickly.

## ATTRACTOR STEP 2
## VISUALIZE

Imagine it with all your senses as if you already have that which you want to attract to your life. You can use magazine cut-outs on a board, words that remind you that this is already yours, or a screen saver in your phone and computer. Just immerse yourself in that which you want to attract so you start integrating its specific energy into your own energy.

## ATTRACTOR STEP 3
## AFFIRM

Use your words and your voice to attract what you want to your life. Write affirmations and say either silently in your mind or give them more strength by saying them aloud. Craft your daily language to attract what you want. Talk as you would if you had manifested what you wanted already. Show the universe you know it's already yours and you have accepted it with arms wide open.

## ATTRACTOR STEP 4
### RAISE YOUR VIBE

Vibe it! Raise your vibratory frequency so you become a magnet for good things including what you want to manifest. Be grateful, love, sing, dance, write, do art, go out for a walk, take some time to help someone in need.

## ATTRACTOR STEP 5
### LET GO

Make space for what you want. As you declutter and get rid of what doesn't serve your best and highest purpose, you'll make space for what you really want to attract to your life. You can practice letting go physically or mentally by being compassionate and practicing discernment instead of judgment.

## ATTRACTOR STEP 6
### ALIGN YOUR ENERGY

Prepare for it. Aligning your energy with what you want to manifest makes it easier for the universe to bring it to you faster. When your aura is healthy and your chakras are open and clear, you become a magnet to opportunities and miracles.

# ATTRACTOR STEP 7
## DO ENERGY WORK

Supercharge it. Doing energy work before doing physical work takes the "heavy lifting" away. Working with light supercharges your manifesting process. The more you work with light, the easier it is to live in balance, thus the easier it is to attract what you want.

# CONGRATULATIONS!

This is the end of the book and the beginning of a new phase in your life. Now you have more tools to continue your journey more consciously. May your life be filled with light, love, and laughter.

Never forget that you are an amazing and powerful being. You have so many gifts and huge potential. It's up to you to embrace them or discard them. You are capable of manifesting beyond your imagination.

The law of attraction is universal and makes no exceptions. No one is excluded, especially you! You have the same power to create what you are dreaming about as someone who has already manifested it.

You can manifest the life that your heart desires!

As we work with the universe to attract amazing things for our life, we can be of great service to our planet by including good intentions for it and all life on Earth. We can manifest a planet with peace, love, light, clean water, clean air, and harmony.

It's been not only a blessing to share this book with you but a divine appointment. I am thrilled we have coincided in this time and space.

Enjoy the ride and trust your own process.

Much love from my heart to yours.

Gertrude Marie

Gertrude Marie is passionate about writing and helping others manifest their dreams. She currently lives in Minnesota, where she writes, teaches and produces courses.

Connect with Gertrude Marie
www.GertrudeMarie.com
Facebook: www.facebook.com/lifeshiftersformula/
Instagram: GertrudeMarieAuthor

## ** HERE'S MY GIFT TO YOU **
Free Manifestation Play Sheet
https://www.gertrudemarie.com/free-play-sheet-1

Made in the USA
Middletown, DE
22 May 2022